DISASTER STRIKES!

THE MOST DANGEROUS SPACE MISSIONS OF ALL TIME

JEFFREY KLUGER

PHILOMEL BOOKS

Also by Jeffrey Kluger

TO THE MOON!

PHILOMEL BOOKS
An imprint of Penguin Random House LLC
New York

Copyright © 2019 by Jeffrey Kluger.

Library of Congress Cataloging-in-Publication Data
Names: Kluger, Jeffrey, author.
Title: Disaster strikes! : the most dangerous space missions of all time /
Jeffrey Kluger. | Description: New York, NY : Philomel Books, [2019] | Audience: Ages 8–12. |
Audience: Grades 4 to 6. | Identifiers: LCCN 2018038095| ISBN 9781984812759 (hardcover)
| ISBN 9781984812766 (e-book) | Subjects: LCSH: Space vehicle accidents—Juvenile literature.
| Manned space flight—History—Juvenile literature. | Outer space—Exploration—History—
Juvenile literature. | Classification: LCC TL867.K58 2019 | DDC 363.12/41—dc23 |
LC record available at https://lccn.loc.gov/2018038095

Printed in the United States of America.
ISBN 9781984812759
1 3 5 7 9 10 8 6 4 2
Edited by Jill Santopolo. • Design by Ellice M. Lee.
Text set in Baskerville.

The stories told in this book are adapted from the *Countdown*
podcast that the author wrote for *Time* magazine.

TO MY DAUGHTERS,
WITH LOVE

CONTENTS

> INTRODUCTION >

TRAVELING IN SPACE might be the most thrilling thing a human being can do—unless, of course, it turns out to be the most horrifying. Just as often, it can wind up being both.

There has never been any form of exploration or travel that is entirely safe. Danger and even death lurk in the crack-up of a car, in the crash of an airplane, in the slow-motion disaster of a sinking ship. Climb a mountain, paddle along a river, merely hike a trail in an unfamiliar wilderness and you expose yourself to at least some kind of risk.

Space is different, though, because space is a place we were not meant to be. Even when you're miles above the ground in a million-pound airplane hurtling along at 500 miles per hour, you're still within the skin of the atmosphere, still contained by the bio-dome of the world, where there is air and water and warmth and life. In space, all that's missing. It's a place of hard vacuum, of killing cold, of blistering radiation. It's a place that can't be reached at all without giant machines that carry millions of pounds of explosive fuel and are able to reach speeds in the tens of thousands of miles per hour.

That's not easy. That's not safe. And that can cost lives.

Since 1961, when Yuri Gagarin, a Russian cosmonaut, became the first human being in space, orbiting the Earth in his *Vostok 1* spacecraft, more than 500 people have followed him aloft on more than 300 different missions. Nine of those missions flew to the moon, carrying twenty-four different Americans, twelve of whom walked on the lunar surface.

Every single one of those astronauts or cosmonauts—or taikonauts, too, now that China has begun its own human space program—has gone aloft knowing the risks involved. But all of them have gone aloft mindful of the singular splendor of the journey, too.

It's not just the weightlessness—the sudden ability to fly, after a lifetime spent as an earthbound creature—though that's a lot of fun. And it's not just the view—the sight of the Earth far below and the vast vault of space above, the stars brilliant, white and strangely untwinkling, since there is no intervening atmosphere to distort the view.

It's the sense of doing something improbable, of touching something untouchable, of being a pioneer. We think nothing of spending twelve hours in an airplane traveling 7,000 miles between New York and Beijing, but we recall in admiration and wonder the twelve-second, 120-foot powered flight that Orville and Wilbur Wright achieved on December 17, 1903, because Orville and Wilbur Wright went first. One day we may all get to take vacation trips to the moon, but they will mean nothing compared to the mere eighty-eight minutes Gagarin spent aloft on his single orbit of the Earth.

It's that sense of going first, of walking point for the whole human species, that drives the men and women who take the risk of flying in space. I once asked Pete Conrad, the commander of *Apollo 12* and the third person to walk on the moon, if he was at least a little anxious the entire time he was on the lunar surface, aware that if the engine of his lunar module didn't fire as it was supposed to and get him back into space, he'd be marooned forever. "Nah," he answered. "I was a happy guy on the moon."

I once similarly asked Jim Lovell, who went to space four times, including two trips to the moon, on *Apollo 8* and *Apollo 13*, if on the last night he was home before all of those trips, he didn't look around his living room and think, *Wow, if something goes wrong, I'll never see this house again.* His answer: "No. If you thought that way, you wouldn't go."

So the men and women who go to space don't think that way—or if they do, they learn ways to shake off those thoughts and to press on with their mission. That, of course, doesn't mean things *won't* go wrong. That doesn't mean the explorers won't face danger. And that doesn't mean that the risk doesn't exist that they will indeed never see their homes again.

There have been many harrowing moments in the long history of human space flight, especially in the earliest years, when the United States and the Soviet Union—the former Russian empire—were competing to be the first nation to put a human being on the moon. The two countries were the world's greatest superpowers and were also bitter rivals. Both were also in possession of thousands of fearsome nuclear weapons, which made the stakes of their rivalry potentially deadly.

The race to the moon was a peaceful way for that competition to play out, but it was still a dangerous game to play. The rushing sometimes made both countries reckless—cutting corners, breaking rules that good engineers and flight planners normally wouldn't break—and they sometimes paid a terrible price for that. Even when the space race was won, however, even in the modern era, when traveling to Earth orbit has come to seem routine, the dangers remain. Space doesn't change just because we think we're familiar with it, that we've gotten good at visiting it. And the dangers that lurk there don't change, either.

There is no way of saying with certainty what the scariest, most dangerous, most heart-stopping missions have been out of the 300-plus that have been flown in the past six decades. But the dozen missions whose stories are told in these chapters are awfully good candidates. There will be many more human space flights to come—including ones that may take us back to the moon and eventually to Mars. And there may be other emergencies and tragedies to rival these twelve.

Danger is an unavoidable part of exploration. But so is adventure and so is excitement and so is the joy of discovery. It's the reason that, even when disaster strikes, we'll keep on exploring all the same.

A marine helicopter attempts to recover Liberty Bell 7. *When the waterlogged spacecraft nearly pulled the helicopter into the ocean, the cable was cut.*

> ONE >

THE TALE OF THE SINKING SPACECRAFT

Liberty Bell 7, 1961

GUS GRISSOM TRIED not to give much thought to the fact that the rocket he was riding to space was built to kill people. Actually, most people at NASA tried not to give that fact much thought.

The rocket didn't have a killer's appearance; it was a sleek, white stalk of a thing, barely eighty-five feet tall, which wasn't much as rockets go. And it didn't have a killer's name. It was called a *Redstone*—or, on days like today, when an American astronaut was aboard, it was a *Mercury-Redstone,* since the pilot, Grissom in this case, was riding in a *Mercury* spacecraft perched on top of the rocket.

That made it a lot easier to forget that the rocket once looked a lot different—a squatter, fatter machine, painted in an alternating black-and-white pattern. And it went by a different name, too. During World War II, it had been called a

V-2—the "V" stood for *vengeance*—and 1,500 of them were launched by the Nazis from northeastern Germany in 1944 and 1945. Most of the V-2s landed in London and the southeast region of England, killing some 7,000 people. That did nothing to change the outcome of World War II, but it did inflict a lot of terror and suffering on Great Britain before the war's end.

But it wasn't 1944 anymore; it was 1961. And Wernher von Braun, the great designer who had invented the V-2 for Germany, was now working for NASA, building rockets for the peaceful exploration of space. If, with a few modifications, the guts of the V-2 could work just fine in a spaceman's rocket, it made no sense to throw it all away and start over. So the terrible V-2 would become the beautiful *Redstone*, and American astronauts—the good guys—would ride them to space.

Gus Grissom's turn atop the once-deadly missile would come in the early hours of July 21, 1961, and his trip to space that day was an exceedingly big thing for the United States even if it was not much of a mission at all, because it was so brief and simple. The flight would be what was known as a suborbital, a little trip that would send the astronaut and his spacecraft to an altitude of about 120 miles, breaking the skin of the atmosphere, entering the darkness of space, then arcing over and plunging back down to the Atlantic just 300 miles east of Cape Canaveral. What's more, two months earlier, astronaut Al Shepard had flown his own suborbital mission, becoming the first American in space. Grissom would be the second—making his flight much less historic.

The entire trip would take just seventeen minutes—from 8:20 a.m. to 8:37 a.m. If you sat down to watch the flight on TV over breakfast—which tens of millions of Americans were planning to do—the great star voyager would be home before you finished your cereal.

Though Shepard had gone first, Grissom would repeat Shepard's feat—and maybe even outdo him.

He would fly higher than Shepard had and land farther out into the ocean, and the spacecraft would be more maneuverable, too. In the five minutes Grissom would have at the top of his arc, when he would be in the true weightless blackness of space, he would fire his thrusters and practice the pitching and rolling and yawing maneuvers astronauts would have to master for the more ambitious journeys that would follow.

Part of the reason his capsule would fly higher would be because it was lighter, thanks to a nifty innovation that would also make the pilot safer. When Shepard's capsule hit the water, it had been up to him to operate the heavy latch that would open the hatch and allow him to exit into the waiting arms and life raft of navy divers.

When Grissom hit the water, that would all be automated. His hatch was held in place by seventy titanium pins running the entire circumference of the opening. The pins were deliberately weakened with a tiny hole—just six one-hundredths of an inch—drilled into each one. A channel running around the opening of the hatch was lined with a mild explosive charge. When it was time for Grissom to exit, he would remove a small safety cover on the inside of the door, pull a pin to arm the explosive charge and then push a plunger. That would ignite the explosive charge, crack the weakened bolts and blow the hatch out into the ocean.

Grissom, as the sole pilot of this new, souped-up spacecraft, had been allowed to decide on its name. He had chosen *Liberty Bell 7*—a suitably patriotic call sign, with the 7 a nod to the nation's seven-man team of astronauts. Shepard, the first American in space, had similarly named his ship *Freedom 7*.

The television networks had been camped out at Cape Canaveral all night preparing for Grissom's flight, and they were there when the sun rose on July 21. *Liberty Bell 7*'s launch had been delayed twice before in the last week due to bad weather, but today it seemed there would be no such problems.

"Once again, you can feel the tension here at Cape Canaveral," NBC correspondent Peter Hackes said. "After having gone through this suspense twice before this week, the weathermen now tell us that barring further unpredicted changes we have go conditions both here and in the recovery area. Astronaut Gus Grissom, the thirty-five-year-old air force captain, is inside the capsule waiting. We're told he's still cool and calm, ready and eager to make the flight, to become the free world's second man in space."

Newscasters liked to talk about the "free world," which was a way to describe the United States and its allies, especially France, the United Kingdom and the other nations of Western Europe. The other part of the world—the one that was considered un-free—was the Soviet Union and its allies in Eastern Europe, including Poland, Romania and Hungary.

The previous April, the Soviet Union had beaten the United States to space, launching cosmonaut Yuri Gagarin on a one-orbit mission around the planet. For now, the best response America could offer was to set our own records with our own astronauts, and Grissom would soon have his chance to contribute to that effort.

As his *Redstone* rocket sat alone on the pad, its 40,000 pounds of ethyl alcohol and liquid oxygen fuel producing plumes of exhaust, a loud horn sounded to indicate the T-minus-two-minute point to launch. An eight-story cherry picker, holding an escape platform next to the hatch that Grissom could use in the event of an emergency, pulled away.

NBC anchorman Frank McGee announced that milestone. "And now the missile stands completely alone," he said.

Viewers at home would hear all of those voices and more on multiple broadcast feeds, but Grissom himself would hear only one. It would come from the capcom, or capsule communicator, a job that today was being filled by Shepard himself. Shepard was known among the astronauts for his spot-on imitation of a popular comedian who had created a character named José Jiménez. One of his favorite sketches was José as a timid astronaut—and Shepard was ready the moment the rocket left the pad.

"This is *Liberty Bell 7*, the clock is operating," Grissom called, confirming that his *Redstone* had lifted off and the mission timer on his instrument panel had begun to move.

"Loud and clear, José, don't cry too much," Shepard answered.

"Okeydoke," said a happy-sounding Grissom, who clearly wasn't anywhere close to tears. "It's a nice ride up to now."

And it kept being nice, too. The *Redstone* might trace its genes to a weapon of war, but today it was a sweet machine, accelerating Grissom from a standing start to more than 5,000 miles per hour in less than two minutes and carrying him to an altitude of more than 100 miles less than three minutes later.

"I see a star!" Grissom exclaimed as he exited the atmosphere. It was a star in a sky that just minutes before had been a Florida morning to him.

And still Grissom kept climbing, until explosive bolts connecting his spacecraft to the *Redstone* fired. The capsule flew on, leaving the *Redstone*, which had performed faithfully, peacefully and well, to tumble back to Earth, break apart and splash harmlessly into the ocean.

Shortly after and more than twenty miles higher still, Grissom's *Liberty Bell 7* began to surrender to the pull of the Earth, too, arcing slowly over and beginning its return plunge. That was when the fun would come. In those few minutes at the top of the capsule's climb, the pull of gravity was neutralized, and Grissom experienced the singular feeling of weightlessness.

"We are at zero-g and turning around," he called down to Earth. For an astronaut, that was an exciting announcement. Zero-g means no gravity; Grissom was weightless, and if he could have gotten out of his seat in the tiny spacecraft, he would have floated.

He looked around his cockpit and noticed the odd bits of debris—a screw, a washer, a scrap of paper—that were inevitably left behind in even the most painstakingly maintained space-craft and showed themselves only when gravity vanished and they drifted up into view.

"There's a lot of stuff floating around here." He laughed. Then he looked out his window at the Earth below. "It's such a fascinating view out the window, you just can't help but look that way," he said.

"I understand," said Shepard, with an authority no other American had.

What both Shepard and Grissom understood, too, was that the clock on Grissom's instrument panel was still ticking and he would have only a couple more minutes in this fleeting trip to space, so he grabbed his thruster handle and began trying a bit of actual flying.

The thrusters worked, but they were sluggish, and while Grissom could dance his capsule about in multiple directions, it was slow going—the kind of thing he'd been sent up here to learn and the kind of thing he'd report when he got home so that future capsules could have the necessary improvements built in.

Grissom soon released the thruster handle and allowed the onboard computer to take control. Its job now was to turn the capsule around and position it so that its blunt bottom, protected by a heat shield, faced forward, preparing for the flaming plunge that was ahead.

Within a few more seconds, that long fall began, and as it did, the gravitational forces began to accumulate, subjecting both spacecraft and astronaut to a load that would climb to 10 g's, meaning that gravity would be pulling on them with ten times the force it does on Earth. Grissom, who weighed little more than 150 pounds on Earth, would feel as if he weighed 1,500 pounds. The astronauts used to joke that it was like a gorilla sitting on their chests.

"Got a pitch rate here," he said as his spacecraft refined its position. "Okay, g's are starting to build," he went on. "We're up to six." His voice was strained. "There's nine. There's about ten."

Shepard, who knew that crushing sensation, reassured his friend. "Roger, still sounds good," he said.

The spacecraft plunged through the 40,000-foot mark— or about seven miles up, falling like the dead, one-ton weight it was. Then it reached 35,000, then 30,000, and then finally, at 25,000 feet, about forty seconds after the drop had begun, the small, orange-and-white braking parachute, called the drogue chute, deployed and reefed and bloomed—barely seven minutes after the spacecraft had been at the peak of its flight. The chute jerked Grissom back in his seat. But that was a comforting feeling. The drogue chute was needed to slow the spacecraft down enough that a much bigger main parachute could open next. If the capsule were falling too fast, the main parachute could tear.

"There's the drogue," he exclaimed.

At 13,000 feet, the main parachute followed, and now there was nothing to do but wait for the gentle descent to the ocean. Grissom could see the parachute through his window, noticed a small triangular tear in it and reported that to the ground, too—another important observation that would help improve the ship for future trips.

Now he could see the water rising up to meet him, feel the slight swaying as the warm Atlantic winds caught his spacecraft, and then, a moment later, the man who'd been in space ten minutes earlier felt the unmistakable thump of striking the ocean and saw a splash of water wash over his porthole window.

A new voice—one that wasn't that of his fellow astronaut Shepard—filled his headset. He could hear the whup-whup sound of helicopter blades in the background.

"*Liberty Bell 7*," said the voice of the pilot of the rescue chopper. "We have your entry into the water. We will be over you in just about thirty seconds."

Gus Grissom could now allow himself a smile. One American astronaut had flown a perfect suborbital flight. Now two American astronauts had done it. And as for the bad luck of flying a rocket that had as murderous a past as the *Redstone*? Well, that rocket had already hit the ocean and vanished to the bottom, and Grissom was safely floating on the surface, so that was the end of those silly superstitions.

Grissom knew what the drill was now, and it was mostly housekeeping. He had to note and record all of the switch positions on his instrument panel, and he had to ensure that the data-recording equipment that the doctors and engineers would want to examine after the capsule was recovered was in its proper postflight configuration. That would take a few minutes, and while it would be nice to get outside, feel the Atlantic breezes and be choppered aboard the deck of the recovery ship, the USS *Randolph*, he still had work to do.

"Give me how much longer it will be before you get here," he called to the recovery helicopter.

"We are around the capsule now," the pilot answered.

"Roger," Grissom answered. "Give me about five more minutes to mark these switches here, before I call you to come in and hook on."

The business of "hooking on" would be the first critical part of the recovery. The helicopter would fly overhead, lower a grappling hook and snag a bracket at the top of the capsule to stabilize it and prevent it from sinking. Then navy divers from a second chopper would leap in the water and inflate a life raft, Grissom would blow the hatch and they'd help him into the raft. A horse collar from that copter would be lowered to haul him aboard. The divers would follow him up, and they'd all fly back to the deck of the *Randolph*. The first copter would then lift the capsule and bring it aboard the ship, too.

That is exactly how it started to work out. But whatever dark magic may have attended the mission at its beginning and seemed to have passed with the end of the *Redstone* was apparently still lurking about.

Grissom finished recording his switch positions, then removed his helmet and disconnected his oxygen hose, freeing his suit from its remaining tether to the spacecraft. He prepared the hatch for the detonation sequence, removing the plunger cover and the arming pin but taking care not to touch the plunger itself—all according to the flight plan. He leaned to his left, safely away from the hatch, to retrieve a survival-kit knife that he wanted to keep as a souvenir, after which he would call the helicopter to hook on.

At that moment, however, he heard a loud bang. He turned to his right and saw that his hatch was suddenly, smokingly gone—its explosive powder having detonated, its weakened bolts having fractured and the entire thing having blown itself into the ocean, even though the plunger had remained untouched.

The surging Atlantic stretched just outside the opening, and Grissom prepared to alert the rescue helicopter to hook on and fast, but before he could do that, the capsule rolled in the waves, and seawater began pouring in through the door.

The spacecraft's interior was tiny, just sixty cubic feet—far smaller than a phone booth—and the water would fill it fast. When it did, the capsule would sink, with Grissom inside. He did the only thing he could do in that moment, which was to tumble out of the hatch and into the ocean.

The crews aboard the two helicopters hovering overhead saw what was happening and instantly moved into position. One of them successfully got the grappling hook onto the spacecraft; the other moved in to rescue Grissom.

But the twin choppers were too close together, and had the blades collided, all of the men on both vehicles, to say nothing of the one in the water, would be killed. What's more, the wind coming off both machines was creating swells that were crashing over Grissom's head.

The helicopter meant to rescue him backed off, and that would normally have been a safe thing to do. Grissom's space suit, even without its helmet, should be watertight, and the air inside that kept it pressurized would serve as a whole-body life preserver.

But in Grissom's case, that wouldn't work. In the emergency evacuation, he had not had time to take two precautions: to roll up the rubberized dam around his neck that would prevent water from flowing into the top of the suit, and to close the oxygen port that had been connected to the hose.

As soon as he hit the water, the suit began filling. In his first seconds in the ocean, he was floating up to about the level of his underarms. Now he felt himself sinking to his shoulders. As one helicopter struggled to lift the capsule, which was becoming heavier and heavier as a result of the seawater flowing inside, Grissom, choking on seawater, waved frantically for the other.

The NBC reporter on the deck of the *Randolph*, peering through binoculars, could see the struggle to hold the spacecraft, but not the peril that was facing Grissom.

"The concern at the moment is with the capsule!" he reported. "The helicopter has a cable on it and is holding it at the present time."

The helicopter, however, was losing that fight. It had the muscle to lift the one-ton spacecraft. It could even lift it if the water added a couple hundred pounds. But by now a full ton of water had poured inside. The winch on the helicopter fought to lift the load, but rather than the capsule coming up, the chopper was going down. Its wheels were drawing closer and closer to the water, and then they were actually in it. The splash from the propellers was increasingly swamping Grissom, and the chopper itself was seconds from crashing.

The pilot did the only thing he could do, which was to hit the switch that released the spacecraft, sending it on an anvil-like plunge to the seafloor three miles below.

"The capsule has been dropped!" the NBC man called. "That is going to be a big problem. The capsule contains very important information, and they want that very, very badly."

But the capsule was expendable. Grissom himself was very close to following his spacecraft down. He vanished briefly under the water, fighting the waves and the increasing weight of his suit, disappearing and reappearing as the other helicopter approached, closer and closer, creating even worse waves, but that couldn't be helped now.

A horse collar was dropped, and Grissom, with the last of his strength, lifted his arms and slipped through it. The collar had come down backward, which forced him to put it on that way, but it would hold for the short hoist to the helicopter. A moment later he was on board the chopper, and a few minutes after that, he was on the *Randolph*. He emerged from the helicopter drenched and spent, but smiling.

Not long after, unnoticed by the TV crews and even many of the sailors, the other helicopter, carrying nothing at all, landed, too.

There would be those who claimed Grissom panicked and hit the hatch release plunger too early, but nothing in his laconic voice on the tapes of the air-to-ground conversations suggested anything of the kind. There would be those who claimed he accidentally bumped the switch when he reached to get his souvenir knife or moved around to perform another post-exit job. But the capsule had been designed with the plunger positioned to prevent that, and the problem had never presented itself in earlier rehearsals.

The best guess in the investigation that followed was that a flaw in the hatch, perhaps an errant spark or charge of some kind, had caused the explosives to blow on their own.

Grissom would be officially cleared of error in the incident, and he would be assigned to another mission—flying as commander of *Gemini 3*, the first flight of NASA's two-person ships—in 1965. He would playfully nickname that spacecraft *The Unsinkable Molly Brown*, after the Broadway musical.

In 1999, a salvage expedition recovered his *Liberty Bell 7* spacecraft from beneath 15,000 feet of Atlantic water. The survival knife was still aboard.

The uncrewed Agena *spacecraft seen from the right-hand window of* Gemini 8.
The two vehicles would successfully dock—but almost nothing would go well after that.

〉 TWO 〉

SPINOUT IN SPACE

Gemini 8, 1966

NEIL ARMSTRONG DIDN'T believe in omens, but he got a nasty one anyway the moment he climbed into his *Gemini 8* spacecraft on the morning of March 16, 1966. As it turned out, if Armstrong had believed in omens, he might have been better prepared for what the rest of the day held for him.

Armstrong had been in a *Gemini* spacecraft plenty of times before; he'd been an astronaut for four years now and had done an awful lot of training in the new, two-person spacecraft. By any measure it was a hot rod of a ship—so much bigger than the little one-person pod that was the *Mercury* spacecraft, and so much more maneuverable, too. You could ride in a *Mercury*— but you could fly a *Gemini.*

Today, Armstrong, the commander of the Gemini 8 mission, was scheduled to do a lot of flying. Halfway across Cape Canaveral, an *Atlas* rocket was standing and steaming on launchpad fourteen, ready to take off for orbit carrying an unmanned spacecraft called an *Agena*.

The *Agena* was a beast: a twenty-six-foot-long, three-and-a-half-ton satellite, carrying four more tons of explosive fuel. It had a rocket engine at one end and a docking port at the other.

At 10:00 a.m., the *Atlas* would blast off and carry the *Agena* to orbit. Just 100 minutes later, Armstrong, a rookie, and his copilot, Dave Scott, another first-timer, would take off and give chase. Finding the *Agena* in orbit, they would move in close and then dock the nose of their ship in the port of the target.

A maneuver like that had never been accomplished before—and that was a problem. Getting astronauts back from the moon would require just this kind of piloting finesse, since a lunar module leaving the lunar surface would have to find the *Apollo* mother ship waiting in orbit and successfully link up with it. If it couldn't, the astronauts would never make it home.

On launchpad nineteen, as Armstrong and Scott eased into the seats of their *Gemini* ship, which itself sat atop their eleven-story *Titan* rocket, fellow astronaut Pete Conrad helped them get settled in. His job at the moment was to fasten the clasps on the escape parachutes the crew would use if an emergency during launch required them to eject.

One of Armstrong's clasps, however, wouldn't close. Conrad peered at it and frowned.

"It's glue, Neil," he said.

Armstrong responded incredulously: "Glue?" he asked.

"Glue," Conrad repeated. Somehow, a technician or other member of the ground crew had dripped a glob of glue inside the workings of the latch. If it couldn't be cleared, *Gemini 8* couldn't fly. If *Gemini 8* couldn't fly, neither could the *Agena*. Two launches would be scrubbed because of a tenth of a teaspoon of goo that had somehow found its way into the wrong spot.

Conrad, trained in every single bit of the *Gemini* system, used the most low-tech tool he had at his disposal—his finger—to try to gouge out the mess. After multiple tries, he did it. Armstrong tested the clasp several times, flashed a thumbs-up and the flight was a go.

The relief in Mission Control was palpable, partly because this mission had a lot more riding on it than just its planned dance with the *Agena*, and the shoulder patch the astronauts designed as the emblem for their flight captured that—provided you could make any sense out of it. The patches for all of the other *Gemini* flights had featured some variation on the spacecraft and the mission number and the names of the astronauts. Armstrong and Scott chose, instead, a pair of stars projecting a beam of light that burst into a rainbow of colors.

The star part made sense—maybe. There were two of them, so they must have represented the astronauts. But the rainbow? That, NASA explained when reporters asked—and plenty of them did—stood for the fact that this was a full-spectrum mission. There would be the rendezvous and docking, yes, but there would also be a suite of ten scientific experiments to conduct, plus two space walks by Scott. In fact, one of the space walks would be so long—a full ninety minutes—that it would last for an entire orbit.

The newspapers had fun with that one, running headlines that read: DAVE SCOTT WILL BE THE FIRST MAN TO WALK AROUND THE WORLD!

The mission would last only three days, but a lot would be packed into that short time, and it all started off perfectly when the *Atlas-Agena* left launchpad fourteen precisely on time at 10:00 a.m. and raced to a near-circular orbit 146 miles up.

The *Gemini* spacecraft—with its little glue problem sorted out—followed 101 minutes later, and Armstrong and Scott were clearly enjoying the ride.

"Hey, how about that view!" Scott enthused as the rocket climbed.

"That's fantastic!" Armstrong answered, and then added, "Boy! Here we go!"

And there they went indeed. Less than ten minutes after leaving the launchpad in Florida, the astronauts were in orbit.

What followed would be six hours of some of the most pains-taking work the two crewmen had ever done, with Armstrong tweaking various combinations of the sixteen little thrusters arrayed around the ship, until slowly, over four complete orbits, they closed in on the *Agena*—though they still couldn't see it.

Finally, when the two spacecraft were just seventy-six miles apart, the astronauts saw something reflecting back at them.

Scott warned that it might just be a planet.

Mission Control said that it could be the star Sirius.

But it wasn't a planet and it wasn't Sirius, and as Armstrong and Scott grew closer and closer, the target grew bigger and brighter and revealed itself unmistakably as the

Agena spacecraft—a beautiful machine, precisely launched and waiting exactly where it was supposed to be.

Armstrong, at the controls of his *Gemini*, was having the time of his life.

"Man, it flies easy. I'd love to let you try it!" he said to Scott.

"I'll get my chance. It's up to you; you stick with it," Scott encouraged.

The *Gemini* edged closer and closer to the *Agena*, as Armstrong released mere breaths of propellant from his thrusters. Both spacecraft were moving at matching speeds of 17,500 miles per hour, but the *Gemini* could speed up or slow down by a few inches per second, which is all it takes in the business of docking in space.

"Okay, we're sitting at two feet out," Armstrong called as he began to close the final distance.

He then crept forward until he was just a foot away, and then just a few inches, and then the front of the *Gemini* settled into the port of the *Agena* and the docking latches snapped shut.

"Flight, we are docked!" Armstrong called.

In Mission Control, where the loudest sound was usually that of men murmuring into headsets, a chorus of whoops and cheers rang out as they hadn't since the very first American space flights.

NASA was one very big step closer to the moon.

Still, there were reasons to be wary—and the people at NASA knew it. The *Agena* might be a beautiful machine, but it was also known to be a temperamental one, given to occasional bouts of misbehavior, and that included problems with its engine and thrusters. While a certain degree of imperfection was acceptable in a spacecraft that wasn't carrying astronauts, it could be deadly when that spacecraft was linked up with another ship that was carrying them.

What's more, Mission Control wouldn't always know if something had gone awry in the ships. American spacecraft orbiting Earth were not in constant touch with the ground in Florida; rather, they relied on a necklace of tracking stations around the world—in California, Mexico, Bermuda, Australia, Hawaii and elsewhere. Between those radio footprints, there were long minutes of blackout.

At the Tenerife station in the Canary Islands, astronaut Jim Lovell, who was manning the communications console, knew as well as anyone else the risks Armstrong and Scott faced as they flew through their orbits still linked to the target vehicle. So he radioed up a warning.

"If you run into trouble and the attitude control system of the *Agena* goes wild, just turn it off and take control with the spacecraft," he said. The attitude referred to the direction the spacecraft was pointing. If that control system went wild, it meant the ship could tumble around, completely out of control.

Armstrong promised he would do just that. Then he and Scott slipped into blackout.

There was little for the crew to do in the fifteen minutes before reacquisition of signal. There would be no maneuvering while they were out of contact with the ground, so the time would be spent simply keeping the spacecraft at a stable attitude and perhaps resuming a meal they had begun in the six hours they had been chasing the other ship.

As Scott tried to finish perfectly terrible chicken and gravy served in a plastic pouch, and a dessert of brownies, he gazed out his window. It was entirely dark outside, since the astronauts were on the nighttime side of the planet, so there was no horizon below them to see. That made it hard to determine if their ship was remaining stable.

Scott glanced at the instrument panel at what was known as the eight ball—the attitude indicator that spun in all axes in response to any movement of the ship.

It was supposed to be stationary. It wasn't.

"Neil, we're in a bank," he said.

Armstrong glanced at the eight ball. Scott was right, only it was worse than a bank. The *Gemini-Agena* combination was drifting in two axes—both roll and yaw, which meant a spin around its nose-to-tail axis, as well as a rotation in its left-right orientation. The only thing missing was a pitch—or a head-over-heels tumble.

This had to be the *Agena*—the piece-of-junk *Agena*—causing exactly the kinds of trouble Lovell had warned them about. The smart move here was the one Lovell had recommended, and it actually involved two moves. Armstrong made them both.

First, he took hold of his attitude controller and used the thrusters on the *Gemini* to try to bring the two-ship assembly to heel. That worked—sort of—but the motion wasn't completely stilled.

So next he sent a command to the *Agena* to shut down its

guidance system completely. *Do nothing*, the manned spacecraft was ordering the unmanned one. *We'll take care of this.*

That seemed to do it. The two ships steadied themselves— but only for a moment. Then the erratic motion resumed. And then it accelerated, a full, three-axis tumble this time. Then it got faster still, which was extremely dangerous.

The worse the tumble became, the more centrifugal energy the two ships were generating, raising the possibility the *Agena* would simply rip away from the *Gemini*, tearing its metal skin and damaging the electronics, to say nothing of the parachutes, packed in the nose. If that happened, the astronauts could never come home.

What's more, the 4,000 pounds of explosive fuel in the *Agena*'s tanks had not gone anywhere. If the problem was being caused by an electrical glitch anywhere in the miles of cabling inside the ship, the possibility existed that it would ignite the tanks. *Gemini 8* had gone into a communications blackout from which it might never emerge.

The only way to save the crew was for Armstrong to hit the DISENGAGE switch, which would undock the two ships, flinging them away from one another. If the problem was a stuck thruster on the *Agena*—which it all but certainly was—he could stabilize his *Gemini*, make a quick jump to a higher orbit and leave it to NASA to command the *Agena* to make a suicide plunge into the atmosphere. With that bad-news spacecraft out of the way, he and Scott could go about the rest of their mission safely.

So Armstrong made that command decision, ordered Scott

to hit the switch that popped the latches and, as soon as that was done, fired a burst from his thrusters to back away fast from the *Agena*.

But the instability only grew worse—a lot worse. The *Gemini*'s tumble increased from a comparatively slow five revolutions per minute up to ten and then quickly to twenty.

Armstrong fought with his attitude controller while Scott threw breaker switches on the instrument panel in front of him, trying to see if the problem might be a bad thruster on the *Gemini*, rather than on the *Agena*. If it was, he could kill the power to that one jet and Armstrong could stabilize the ship with the ones remaining.

None of the breakers Scott tried had any effect, and the tumble increased to thirty RPMs.

"*Gemini 8*, communications check," came a voice in Armstrong's and Scott's headsets as they at last flew into range of the next tracking station, "how do you read?"

"We have serious problems here!" Scott answered. "We're tumbling end over end. We're disengaged from the *Agena*."

"What seems to be the problem?" the ground answered, either not understanding the severity of the emergency or trying too hard to sound calm.

"We're rolling and can't turn anything off," Armstrong said.

"We have a violent left roll," Scott added for emphasis.

That violent roll now increased to forty RPMs. The ground radioed back a "Roger, copy," but that was really all it could do.

Controllers on Earth could not override Armstrong's

thruster maneuvers, and even if they could, they wouldn't. Only a pilot, in the seat, at the controls, feeling the motion as it happened, could respond fast enough to save this spacecraft.

Armstrong kept wrestling with his thrusters as Scott kept looking for a faulty breaker and the tumble increased to forty-five RPMs, then fifty and then fifty-five. They were closing in on sixty—or one revolution in multiple axes every second—and that would likely be the end.

Sixty RPMs was the point at which the integrity not only of the spacecraft would be threatened, but of the astronauts themselves. That was when even pilots who had spent countless hours training in centrifuges would notice the first signs of vertigo setting in—the tunnel vision, the inability to orient, and finally the unconsciousness that would follow. With that, there would be no controlling force of any kind in charge of the spacecraft.

Already the dizziness was beginning and darkness was creeping in at the periphery of the astronauts' visual field.

Armstrong knew what he had to do.

"All we've got left is the reentry control system!" he shouted to Scott.

That might be the best answer, but it also came at a very high price.

Shutting down the main thrusters and going to the ones used during reentry was a one-way decision. The moment they did that, NASA rules decreed that they had to come home. They'd need the reentry thrusters to survive the plunge through the atmosphere at the end of the mission. If they used them now and then continued to fly for three more days, the fuel could clog and freeze the lines.

The mission, however, was no longer the thing that was on the line. The lives of the astronauts were.

"Press on!" Scott answered.

Armstrong did, killing his main thrusters, engaging his reentry system and slowly reducing the spin from deadly to serious, and finally back to manageable.

"We're regaining control of the spacecraft," Scott reported to the ground.

"Roger, copy," the ground responded.

And that, the ground didn't have to add, was that.

There would be no suite of experiments conducted. There would be no space walk—never mind two. Dave Scott would not become the man who walked around the world.

"I have some reentry data when you are ready to copy," the Hawaii tracking station said forlornly.

"Go ahead," Armstrong answered, revealing as little disappointment in his voice as he could.

Less than three hours after that—or only ten hours, forty-one minutes and twenty-six seconds into what was supposed to be a seventy-two-hour flight—*Gemini 8* splashed down in the Pacific Ocean.

NASA would later conclude that thruster number eight on the *Gemini* spacecraft had, as the engineers put it, failed open— it had switched itself on and nothing could turn it off.

The *Agena* had flown flawlessly. It was the *Gemini* that had gone wrong.

Three years and four months later, Neil Armstrong, survivor of Gemini 8, would serve as commander of *Apollo 11*, becoming the first human being to walk on the moon.

Two years after that, Dave Scott, the commander of *Apollo 15*, would become the seventh.

Gemini 8 might have been lost, but smart thinking by its crew allowed later history to be made.

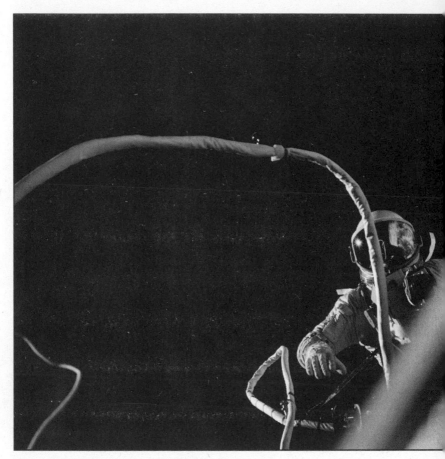

Astronaut Gene Cernan, connected by his umbilical cord, during his Gemini 9 *spacewalk. It looks like fun; it wasn't.*

❯ THREE ❯

THE TERRIBLE, HORRIBLE, NO-GOOD, VERY BAD SPACE WALK

Gemini 9, 1966

GENE CERNAN HAD no reason to think he'd get a chance to fly on *Gemini 9*. For any pilot with any ambition, that was a shame.

Gemini 9, which was supposed to launch sometime in May of 1966, was going to be a sweet mission. It would last only three days, but they would be three very busy ones—the *Gemini 9* would take care of all of the experiments that the *Gemini 8* didn't get a chance to perform because of the faulty thruster. There would be the steeplechase with the *Agena* target vehicle—the unmanned spacecraft would blast off just hours ahead of the *Gemini* and would be waiting in orbit when the astronauts got there. Just as with the *Gemini 8*, their job would be to find it and catch up with it in the millions of cubic miles of Earth-orbital space and then dock with it—executing an in-formation linkup that would be critical for the Apollo lunar missions down the road. The last time that kind of maneuver had been attempted, it had ended in disaster. This time, the NASA flight planners were confident they could get it right.

More thrilling would be what would happen on the third day of the mission, when the copilot, in the right-hand seat, would step out into space and spend more than three hours jetting around on a backpack at the end of a 150-foot tether—the kind of maneuver no American astronaut or Soviet cosmonaut had ever attempted before.

Three hours would mean two full orbits—one more than Scott had been planning to attempt on *Gemini 8*—and if there was a better way to spend two full laps around the planet than flying all but free in space, it was hard to think of one.

But Cernan hadn't gotten the nod for the right-hand seat in *Gemini 9*. That had gone to his friend Elliot See, a rookie who, like Cernan himself, had not yet had his first flight. Elliot would be flying under the command of Charlie Bassett, another first-timer. Cernan, meantime, had been paired with commander Tom Stafford, as the *Gemini 9* backup crew. They'd study and train as hard as the prime crew—but unless an illness or injury intervened, the backups would go nowhere at all, waving good-bye on launch day like any other person stuck on the planet.

Still, there were compensations. If there was any astronaut in NASA Cernan didn't mind understudying, it was Elliot See, a smart, tough, genial rookie who had worked hard and earned his spot on this mission.

As the joyride of *Gemini 9* got closer and closer, the names Bassett and See popped up on TVs more and more, but none of the four astronauts got to see much of that coverage, consumed as they were with preparing for the mission. Recently, a lot of that work had involved flying back and forth between the Manned Spacecraft Center in Houston and the McDonnell Douglas aircraft plant in St. Louis, where the *Gemini* spacecraft were built.

One morning at the end of February, just three months before the mission, all four astronauts were expected in St. Louis and they took off early, at 7:35, so that they would have as much time as possible at the factory. It was a good day to fly if you were taking off from Houston but a lousy day if you were landing in St. Louis, where the sky was leaden, low and full of freezing rain.

The astronauts flew as astronauts always flew, in two-seat T-38 jets. Bassett and See took off first, with See in the front seat doing the piloting and Bassett in the back. Stafford and Cernan followed close behind—Stafford up front, Cernan in the rear.

Bassett and See's plane had a little luggage pod attached, so all four men stashed their bags there—including their NASA IDs.

By the time the planes reached St. Louis, the cloud ceiling was down to just 400 feet and the visibility was terrible. Stafford and Cernan could spot Bassett and See intermittently through holes in the clouds, but both planes were flying mostly on instruments.

At one point when the T-38s were nearing the airport, Cernan did glimpse the lead plane, and he didn't like what he saw. Elliot See seemed to be misjudging his approach, coming in high and fast above the runway, which was all wrong, especially in such sketchy weather.

What the situation called for was breaking off the landing, swinging back around the field and trying the approach again. That's exactly what Stafford began doing in the seat in front of Cernan. In the lead plane, however, See apparently had other ideas, banking sharply low and left and vanishing into the soup below.

"Where the hell is he going?" Stafford barked.

Cernan had no answer to that question as Stafford peeled off and climbed, and as it turned out there never would be an answer.

In the seconds that followed, witnesses on the ground would report seeing Bassett and See's T-38 appear suddenly through the ceiling of clouds, far too close to the ground for a safe landing. It circled once around the air traffic control tower, and then fired its afterburners, apparently trying to gain altitude. That might have worked a few seconds earlier and a few hundred feet higher, but now it was too late.

With a titanic sound and a blinding flash, the T-38 smashed squarely into the high, hard wall of Building 101—the very building in which the *Gemini*s were built—and exploded into a fireball. The building and the spacecraft inside survived the hit; the aircraft and its crew didn't.

Up in the sky, making safe circles and repeatedly asking the tower for permission to land, Stafford and Cernan knew none of this.

Half an hour later, they were finally cleared to approach,

but they landed far enough from the flames at Building 101 that they could not see them through the fog.

They suspected something was terribly wrong only when the air traffic controller hailed them.

"What are the pilots' names in NASA nine-zero-seven?" he called, citing the tail number of their plane.

Cernan, puzzled, answered. "Stafford and Cernan," he said.

"Roger," the controller answered, never explaining that there was simply not enough left of the men who had been in NASA nine-zero-one to allow them to be identified, and that if there had been any personal effects aboard the plane—luggage, say, or NASA IDs—they had been destroyed, too.

It would only be after Stafford and Cernan taxied closer to the building and saw the fire and the wreckage that they learned all that—and learned, too, that *Gemini 9* was now theirs.

It was an assignment that had come to the men only as a result of two lost lives. Before the mission was over, it would come very close to claiming Cernan's life, too.

If *Gemini 9* started off under a curse, the bad fortune seemed determined to stick around. Launch day arrived on May 17, and Stafford and Cernan climbed inside their *Gemini* spacecraft on launchpad nineteen at Cape Canaveral; the *Agena* spacecraft atop its *Atlas* rocket stood ready over on launchpad fourteen. The *Atlas* lifted off first and seemed to be functioning smoothly. But just minutes into its flight, it exploded, raining debris in the nearby Atlantic. With no *Agena* to chase, Stafford and Cernan would have nothing to do for two-thirds of their three-day mission. They were thus extracted from their spacecraft and would have to wait to fly another day.

That day came on June 1. NASA did not have a flight-ready *Agena* available, but it did have a substitute called the ATDA, for the augmented target docking adapter. Whatever name NASA had for the thing, the astronauts simply called it "the Blob"—a nod to its simple design and its stubby eleven-foot length.

Its silly nickname aside, the Blob did what the *Agena* didn't, which was get to space. But this time the astronauts' rocket was the one that failed, with an onboard computer crashing and once again scrubbing the launch.

Finally, on June 3, with the Blob waiting in orbit, the launch was attempted again. When Stafford and Cernan climbed into their cockpit for their third try, they found a piece of paper taped to the instrument panel, left by Jim Lovell and Buzz Aldrin, who were now the backups. There was a little poem on the paper that read:

We were kidding before
But not anymore,
Get yourselves into space
Or we'll take your place.

Getting into space was exactly what the astronauts would finally do. At 8:39 a.m., the engines lit and *Gemini 9* at last left the launchpad.

"We're on the way! The clock has started!" exulted Stafford

after a glance at the mission clock on the instrument panel confirmed the liftoff.

"Beautiful, Tom! We're going!" Cernan answered.

Eight minutes later, they were in orbit. But in short order, the mission's brief good fortune would turn bad yet again.

Stafford and Cernan spent the better part of their first three orbits successfully chasing down the ATDA, but when they at last caught up to it, something was clearly wrong.

It looked nothing like a spacecraft; it looked nothing like a blob. What it did look like was some kind of animal.

During launch, a protective nose cone had covered one end of the vehicle. Once it got to orbit, a pair of straps were supposed to pop open with the aid of explosive bolts, causing the nose cone to split into two halves like a jaw and fall away, exposing the docking port. Only the forward-most of the two straps popped as it was supposed to, however, causing the jaw to hang open and gape.

"I've got a weird-looking machine here," Stafford radioed down to Mission Control.

"What does it look like?" the ground asked.

"It looks like an angry alligator," Stafford said.

The press absolutely loved that, and no sooner were the words out of Stafford's mouth than editors started writing their "angry alligator" headlines. NASA was not remotely pleased. As long as the leering mouth of the nose cone was there, a docking would be impossible.

A lot of ideas for fixing the problem were tossed around in Mission Control: perhaps Stafford could nudge the jaws with the nose of the *Gemini*—a reasonable thought except that the nose of the *Gemini* was exactly where the spacecraft's parachutes were stowed. Damage them and the crew could never come home.

Perhaps, then, Cernan could take his space walk early, float over to the jaws and see if he could release the cable.

That was another good idea—except for the small problem of the explosive bolt that had not exploded, meaning it could still go at any moment, which could be a very bad thing for Cernan.

Ultimately, it was decided that the docking would be scrubbed. Instead, *Gemini 9* would spend the first two days of its three-day mission playing cat and mouse with the alligator, flying far away from it and then rendezvousing again from above and below, practicing what was the far harder part of the rendezvous and docking exercise anyway.

Finally, on the third day, it was Cernan's chance to take his walk in space, and he knew that the experience would be a lot more challenging than most people realized.

The challenges would start with the backpack Cernan was going to use. It was technically known as the astronaut maneuvering unit, or AMU, and one important thing differentiated it from backpacks used by stunt fliers on Earth: the ones on Earth were powered by nitrogen, which does not explode or burn easily; the AMU used pressurized hydrogen peroxide, which was real rocket fuel. The jets through which the exhaust would be expelled ran between the astronaut's legs.

That seemed like a very bad idea for a very basic reason,

so a sort of chain-mail layer was added to the lower half of the already heavily layered space suit. Cernan playfully called that addition his chrome pants, but there was nothing terribly funny about the way they limited his maneuverability.

Cernan would not exit the spacecraft already wearing his AMU, since there was not enough room for it in the cabin. Instead, he would float out of the door connected to the spacecraft by a twenty-five-foot umbilical cord and then crawl along the exterior of the nineteen-foot spacecraft until he reached its back end, which was known as the adapter section, because it was the structure that had attached the spacecraft to the rocket. The section was shaped like an open cone without a point, and it adapted the spacecraft's smaller width to the rocket's larger one.

In an open, recessed area at the rear of the adapter, his AMU backpack would be bracketed in place. He would put it on, disconnect from the umbilical and go flying with the AMU at the end of his 150-foot cable. Both the cable and umbilical were attached to the spacecraft to prevent Cernan from floating away, but the umbilical was shorter. That kept him closer to the ship and steadier, too. The 150-foot cable would mean a wilder ride. But merely by going outside at all, Cernan could face terrible peril.

Back in May, as Cernan and Stafford were suiting up for their first launch attempt, Deke Slayton, the chief astronaut, summoned Stafford for a private talk. The two men disappeared and reappeared a few moments later.

Cernan asked Stafford what that odd scene had been about.

"Everything's fine, Geno. No big deal," was all Stafford said.

But it was actually a very big deal. Slayton, as Stafford much later revealed, had reminded the commander that given the difficulty of squeezing through a small spacecraft hatch while wearing a bulky pressure suit, there was always a possibility that once Cernan was outside, he would not be able to climb back in. If that happened, the commander was to try every conceivable option to save his junior pilot, but if all failed, he was to cut him loose. The *Gemini* spacecraft could not reenter with a hatch open and a man dangling outside, and NASA would not lose two lives if it could save one of them.

Stafford silently resolved that Slayton's order was one he would not obey, preferring to die along with Cernan rather than leave him behind, but he was determined to do everything in his power to make sure things didn't come to that.

When Cernan finally opened his hatch and began to float outside, the possibility of disaster seemed very far away.

"Boy, is it beautiful out here, Tom," he exclaimed, as the porthole-like view through the spacecraft window was now replaced by the completely unobstructed sweep of space.

Smiling and sightseeing, Cernan floated up and out effort-lessly, the thick, gold-colored umbilical cord trailing behind him, and reached for a handrail on the side of the spacecraft that he would use as he made his way to the aft end. Only when he did that did he realize that none of his training had properly prepared him for the strange physics of walking in space.

Cernan had nicknamed the umbilical cord "the snake," because that was precisely what its length and thickness seemed like. But on Earth it was at least a stationary snake. In zero-g, it seemed almost alive.

He moved one way, and the stubborn law of actions having equal and opposite reactions caused the motion to ripple down the length of the umbilical and fling him the opposite way. He grabbed the cable hard to stabilize himself, but that, too, created an opposing force that whipped him even harder.

The more Cernan fought, the worse the uncontrolled motion became, flinging him violently about like a fly-fishing lure at the end of a line. That wasn't just unpleasant; it was exceedingly dangerous, as any one of the random motions could slam him hard into the side of the spacecraft.

"The snake is all over me," Cernan reported to Stafford. "I can't get where I want to go."

And Isaac Newton and his laws of motion weren't through with Gene Cernan. The motion of the comparatively small, 170-pound human at the end of the cable was actually beginning to affect the position of the four-ton ship, tipping it off center.

"You're really changing the moment of the inertia of the spacecraft," Stafford warned, using a technical term that could not conceal the seriousness of what he was saying.

The spacecraft had to stay stable to remain in radio contact with Earth and to keep Cernan's umbilical from getting tangled further. The only way to damp out the motion of the ship was for Stafford to fire his thrusters, which he dared not do when Cernan was outside.

Cernan did his best to stay as still as he could, at last taking hold of the spacecraft and creeping hand over hand down its length. The work was extremely slow going, and even in the deep freeze of space, he began to become badly overheated. He noticed a faint fogging on the inside of his visor—not enough to obscure his view, but enough to dim it. His heart began trip-hammering at 155 beats per minute—twice his healthy average.

When he at last reached the end of the ship, still more trouble loomed. The adapter section had been attached to the rocket by the same type of explosive bolts the straps on the target vehicle used. In this case, the bolts had blown successfully, but they had left behind a jagged sawtooth of sharp edges all along the adapter section's circular rim, like the ragged end of an open can. A single scrape could slice a space suit completely open.

Cernan carefully floated out and around the blades and back into the open end of the adapter. That circular space was ten feet in diameter and resembled nothing so much as a giant wok covered in reflective gold foil. Like a wok it, too, could focus and magnify heat—and the raw sun streaming onto the ship provided plenty of that. In the center of the big, open dish was the AMU.

Maneuvering himself inside, Cernan backed into the jet pack and began putting it on as he had practiced in the simulated zero-g airplane on Earth. But here, too, nothing worked as it should. The armrests that held the controls would not extend; the shoulder harnesses were impossible to manipulate. The knobs to power up the system would not turn; instead, as Cernan tried to twist them he began to rotate—Newtonian physics still working its mischief. The mere business of freeing the backpack from the bracket was proving impossible as well, as the latches that held it would not open.

All the while, the unfiltered sunlight baked the foil adapter.

"We're really cooking back here," Cernan said to Stafford.

"Okay, just take your time, Gene," Stafford responded.

That, however, was something Cernan could not do. NASA had budgeted three hours; one hour was already gone and he would not get more. So he wrestled with the AMU, working even harder and causing his visor to fog completely. He strained his head as far forward as he could in the helmet and wiped a small spot clear with the tip of his nose, providing a little keyhole of sight that he knew would not last. The heat he was producing and the CO_2 he was exhaling were simply overwhelming the space suit's environmental system.

His heart rate, which had already alarmed the flight surgeon in Houston when it broke 155, now galloped to 160, then 170, then 180, the threshold at which loss of consciousness can result.

Adding to all of that, an unknown malfunction began causing the communications link between the astronauts to fail, with static overwhelming half of what the two men tried to say to each other. Stafford did his best to shout through the noise and monitor his copilot's welfare.

"Is the visor starting to clear?" he called.

"If I don't breathe," Cernan answered.

"But I don't recommend that," Stafford said.

Cernan allowed himself a small, grim laugh, but Stafford

had had enough. He keyed open his microphone and hailed the tracking station in Hawaii, which was currently below the ship.

"Hawaii, would you relay to Houston for me?" he said.

"Roger, go ahead," the ground answered. Stafford then let loose.

"We had about four or five times more work than we anticipated," he began. "The pilot's visor is completely fogged over. Our communications are poor. He can't get the AMU harnesses hooked up. If it doesn't clear up right away, I'm calling it no go."

"Roger," the ground answered without objection. "Copy."

Stafford gave it three more minutes and checked once more on Cernan's condition, which had gotten worse to the point that he could no longer even see the pressure gauge on the AMU that would monitor the jet pack's thrust. Flying the thing like that would be a madman's act. Stafford made his decision.

"I'm giving the pilot a no go on AMU," he announced.

"Okay, we have that," the ground responded.

"Wait a minute, Tom, I want to try one more time," said Cernan, who had been listening in.

But there would be no one more time, and Cernan knew it. The commander made the call, the ground accepted it and that was that. Slowly, he abandoned the AMU, eased his way around the jagged adapter edge and crept back along the spacecraft to the invitingly open hatch.

When he got there, Cernan slipped his legs into the spacecraft and worked to shimmy back down into his seat, but now he found that the chrome pants and the rigidly inflated suit made it impossible to bend fully.

It would be easier to sit down and shut the hatch if he could let a little air out of his space suit, but it would be suicide to let air out of the space suit if he didn't sit and shut the hatch first. That was precisely the kind of deadly circle Slayton had worried about when he spoke with Stafford before the first launch attempt.

Finally, Cernan did the only thing he could do, which was to force himself to bend—with every hard fold of the suit pressing into his flesh like the sharp edge of a board. He managed a half crouch, gritting his teeth and pulling down on the hatch above his head until the first tooth of its locking device caught. He twisted the latch until the next tooth and the next and the next clicked into place.

"If we can't pressurize the spacecraft in a hurry and I have to stay in this position the rest of the flight, I'll die," he hissed to Stafford.

The hatch finally did get closed and sealed, and as fast as Stafford could, he pressurized the spacecraft. Both men removed their helmets in relief, and Stafford tried to smile. Cernan looked grim.

"I can tell you one thing, Tom," he said. "Once I was back there, my chances were about fifty-fifty."

"More like seventy-thirty," Stafford said encouragingly. Cernan shook his head in disagreement—and both men knew he was right.

The next day, Tom Stafford lit his retro-rockets to bring

the flight of *Gemini 9* to a close; less than an hour after that, the spacecraft was bobbing in the Atlantic. When the astronauts were safely aboard the recovery ship and Cernan removed his suit in the sick bay belowdecks, a full quart of water—all of it sweat—poured out. When he stepped on the scale, the doctor recorded that he had lost thirteen and a half pounds over the course of just three days.

Cernan would fly in space two more times after that and walk one more time. That walk, in December of 1972, would not be in the void, but on the Taurus–Littrow highlands of the moon, where he and crewmate Jack Schmitt would live for three days. He took his final step on the lunar surface in the early morning hours of December 14, 1972, before climbing back into his lunar module. After six successful lunar landings, Congress was reluctant to continue spending money for the moon program and canceled it, choosing to build the Earth-orbiting space shuttle instead. No human being has set foot on the moon in all the years since.

Gus Grissom, Ed White and Roger Chaffee pose with a model of their Apollo 1
spacecraft. Their confidence in their ship was tragically misplaced.

> FOUR >

THE FIRE

Apollo 1, 1967

GUS GRISSOM SNEAKED forbidden food into a spacecraft twice in his life. The first time was a joke; the second time turned out to be an omen.

The time it was a joke, Grissom himself didn't actually do the smuggling. It was his copilot, John Young, who was guilty of that small crime. But Grissom was the commander of the ship, so an offense committed by a subordinate was an offense committed by the boss. Either way, the contraband on that occasion was a corned beef sandwich, which Young carried aboard *Gemini 3* during its three-orbit mission in March of 1965.

Young's stunt was half silliness and half pointed commentary—a jab aimed at the terrible prepackaged meals NASA had been giving its astronauts since Americans began flying in space in 1961. During the brief, one-person flights of the *Mercury* program, the food had been bearable; during the far-longer missions of *Gemini*, it would be far worse.

"Where did that come from?" Grissom asked early in the second orbit, after Young reached into his space suit pocket and produced the unsightly, half-flattened sandwich.

"I brought it with me," Young answered. "Let's see how it tastes. Smells, doesn't it?"

In the closed cockpit, the sandwich did smell. And although it didn't taste bad, it released a small starburst of floating crumbs the minute Grissom bit into it, so he wrapped it back up and put it away. When the two men came home, the NASA administrators, who expected mild misbehavior from astronauts, had a good laugh over the prank. The ones who fretted over even the tiniest deviation from protocol scowled, reminding future crews that a mere bread crumb could snag in a switch or foul a filter and thus cause a cascade of problems that could lead to disaster.

The second time Grissom sneaked forbidden food inside a cockpit was more than a year and a half later, on January 22, 1967. That time the spacecraft was actually a simulator—a functional mock-up of the three-person *Apollo* command module. And that time, the food was a lemon.

Grissom and his crewmates, Ed White and Roger Chaffee, had been spending a lot of time in the simulator lately, and just as much in their actual spacecraft—the *Apollo 1* ship that was already mounted atop its *Saturn 1B* booster—in preparation for the crew's February 14 launch.

Whether ship or mere simulator, the *Apollo* had so far

struck most people at NASA as a slapdash machine. It was error-prone and impossible to work with for more than a little while before something broke down. Repairs were made as needed, but they were patchwork jobs—workarounds and fixes were made on top of earlier fixes, rather than anyone doing the harder work of ripping out the offending systems, redesigning them and reinstalling them only when they worked right.

A disgusted Grissom would complain to the technicians, and then he'd complain to the technicians' bosses and then he'd complain to the NASA bosses. They would all confer among themselves and promise Gus that they would fix the problem, and still the junkyard spaceship got no better. So Grissom decided to make his point a different way. That January 22, at the end of another long day of trying to make the *Apollo* work the way it was supposed to, he climbed out of the simulator, reached into his pocket and pulled out a lemon he had plucked from a tree in his backyard for precisely this occasion. He perched the lemon atop the simulator and walked wordlessly away. A lemon might be a harmless thing, but the word is also slang for a broken-down car, one that not only doesn't work properly, but may be too dangerous to drive.

The engineers looked at one another with indulgent smiles. That Gus, always a little prickly.

Grissom had a right to be a lot more than prickly. Both the *Mercury* and *Gemini* spacecraft that had come before the larger *Apollo* had been built by McDonnell Douglas aircraft in St. Louis, and NASA liked the people there just fine. They knew what the space agency needed, delivered what had been ordered and understood that although they might own the factory and employ the workers, NASA was both the customer and the boss.

But McDonnell couldn't come along for *Apollo*. For one thing, the company had its hands full. McDonnell's people had been working at a dead run since 1960, and they did not have the resources to keep the *Gemini* assembly line running and still build the *Apollo*s in time for a landing on the moon before 1970, which President Kennedy had pledged at the beginning of the 1960s. According to NASA, only three months were supposed to elapse between the late 1966 launch of the last Earth-orbital *Gemini* flight and the launch of *Apollo 1*. It was an almost impossible job, and only a company that was not already overworked could accomplish it successfully.

So this time the work went to North American Aviation in Downey, California, which seemed like a very good choice—until it started to seem like something else entirely.

A lot of the North American engineers had learned their craft in the so-called black programs—the classified programs—of the military, which mostly involved building unmanned vehicles, particularly satellites and missiles. It was hard work, performed to fine tolerances, but none of it involved designing systems that would have to keep a man alive. Their missiles, in particular, didn't even have to work terribly long or terribly well; all they had to do was fly from silo to target and blow up when they were supposed to.

As reports of quality control errors in the *Apollo* spacecraft came back to NASA, they eventually found their way up to

Chris Kraft, the director of flight operations. Kraft wanted to get his own set of eyes on the factory floor in Downey, and he chose to send John Bailey, a widely respected rocket engineer who had been with NASA since its founding. Bailey flew out to the factory and spent several days observing the operation.

When he returned, he filed an exceedingly bleak report, detailing each system and subsystem that was a cause for worry. It was his from-the-gut assessment of the operation as a whole, however, that was most worrisome to Kraft.

"This hardware is not very good," he wrote. "The cabling is being stepped on when they work on the spacecraft. There's no protection for it. The people are not very good at checking this thing out. They're not very good at trying to maintain some semblance of the fact that a human being is going to be in this machine. I'm telling you, it's not good."

Even then, NASA didn't listen—or didn't listen much. That 1970 deadline was only getting closer and the space agency was already trying to manage the expectations of a cranky Congress that was growing increasingly reluctant to fund a moon program at the same time it was pouring money into a widening war in Vietnam. The choice for the space agency seemed to be fly now or wait for perfect hardware and fly never.

So the work went on and the spacecraft got built, and to Kraft and others, the only answer was to pick a crew that inspired complete confidence.

Grissom was one of only a handful of men who had been in space twice. He had piloted both the *Mercury* and *Gemini* spacecraft, and each time he had flown an early iteration of the ship and helped wring out its problems. If anyone could manage a balky *Apollo* that still had growing pains, it was him.

White had flown just once, but that time he had made history, becoming the first American to walk in space during the Gemini 4 mission in 1965. He had had a lot of unexpected challenges to overcome during his brief stay outside the spacecraft, including the challenge of squeezing back inside the spacecraft and the muscle it took to close the hatch when the walk was done. He displayed a remarkable steeliness throughout.

Chaffee, the rookie, might not have traveled in space yet, but he knew how to pilot a flying machine and how to stay alive in one even when all manner of forces were conspiring to kill him. In 1962, when the US and USSR had come within an eyeblink of nuclear war over the appearance of ballistic missiles in Cuba, Chaffee had been one of the navy pilots who flew reconnaissance missions over the missile sites. Getting shot down or even chased off could easily have led to a war, but he kept his head and flew his missions and helped the Americans win that stare-down with the Soviets.

Finally, on January 27, 1967—five days after Grissom made the statement with his lemon and just three weeks before the planned launch—the astronauts were scheduled for what was known as a plugs-out test of the launch sequence. The exercise would begin when a fully suited crew climbed inside the *Apollo* atop its rocket. With the spacecraft operating on its own internal power system, the crew and the controllers would perform a complete dress rehearsal of all of the procedures that would unfold until the very moment the engines were lit.

The exercise aimed for as much authenticity as possible, and two steps in particular would ensure that. The first involved the *Apollo*'s atmosphere, which was made up of 100 percent oxygen, as it would be in orbit, instead of the 23 percent oxygen and 77 percent nitrogen mix of Earth's atmosphere. Since humans need only the oxygen to stay alive, designers decided not to outfit the spacecraft with tanks of inert nitrogen, since they would merely add weight.

In the vacuum of space, the oxygen in the cockpit would be pumped to a pressure of slightly less than five pounds per square inch—just a third of the nearly fifteen pounds per square inch found at sea level, but really all that an astronaut needed. On the launchpad, however, the interior pressure would have to be much higher, to prevent the force of the sea-level air from squeezing and damaging the hull of the low-pressure space-craft. So for the plugs-out test, the *Apollo* was inflated all the way up to 16.8 pounds per square inch. If anyone was concerned about the fact that fire loves oxygen—especially pure, high-pressure oxygen—that concern did not cause NASA to halt the test.

The second authentic condition involved the hatch, which, once the astronauts were on their backs and strapped in, was directly behind them, over the center seat, where White sat. In the event of an emergency, Grissom, White and Chaffee would be best served by a hatch they could open in a hurry. That would allow them to tumble out of the ship onto the floor of the white room, the little work space at the end of a swing arm that surrounded the capsule at the top of the gantry tower.

An easy-open hatch, however, would not be suitable for a cockpit with so much internal pressure. For that, engineers designed a double hatch—an inner one and outer one—and sealed it with multiple latches. If a pad emergency occurred, the man in the center seat would open the latches with a ratchet and then detach the inner hatch, pull it in and lay it down on the floor. Only then could he open the outer hatch. The commander, in the left-hand seat, would assist if needed. The *Apollo 1* astronauts had practiced this sequence many times, and no matter how hard or efficiently they worked, it took time.

The night before the plugs-out test, Wally Schirra, another two-time space veteran, who was serving as Grissom's backup for this mission, went out to the launchpad with Grissom and spent some time inside the spacecraft running a few final tests. When he climbed out, he shook his head.

"I don't know, Gus," he said. "There's nothing I can point to, but something about this ship just doesn't ring right."

It was a damning judgment for a pilot to deliver, suggesting a vehicle that didn't have discrete, fixable problems, but sweeping systemic ones.

And then Schirra added a warning: "If you have any problems, I'd get out."

Grissom promised he would.

It was at 2:50 p.m. the next day that the plugs-out test began, after the crew had settled into their seats and the double hatch had been closed and sealed. From the start, the exercise ran slowly and haltingly. The day's most nettlesome problem was one that had occurred in earlier tests, too: balky communications.

White and Chaffee could make out the transmissions coming through their headsets, but only through a storm of static and with a lot of dropped words. Grissom's communications line, for reasons the engineers couldn't seem to discover, was even worse.

Before the exercise began, Deke Slayton, the chief astronaut, had offered to climb into the ship along with the crew and spend the entirety of the test period in the lower equipment bay—the small work space beneath the foot of the couches—to see if he could solve the communications problem. But the plugs-out test was supposed to be as authentic as possible, and since there wouldn't be four men jammed into the three-person ship on launch day, there wouldn't be four men today, either. Instead, Slayton stayed in the Launch Control Center at the Cape, listening as best he could to the garbled communications coming down from the ship.

At 6:20 p.m., an exhausted crew and the exhausted ground teams working at both Cape Canaveral in Florida and Mission Control in Houston got a short break while the technicians worked on the communications breakdown and other glitches.

"How are we going to get to the moon if we can't even talk between three buildings?" Grissom groused, at just a few seconds shy of 6:30 p.m. It was one of the rare moments his voice got through clearly.

An uneventful one minute and fourteen seconds passed, and then controllers in the launch room at Canaveral noticed something strange. Glancing at the *Apollo* on their video monitors, they noticed what appeared to be a shadow moving across one of the spacecraft's small portholes. It was a quick, almost urgent motion—not at all the slow, practiced actions of crew members going through their well-rehearsed work. Motion sensors aboard the ship also detected something amiss.

A moment later, a sound cut through the headsets in both Florida and Houston. It was Chaffee shouting, "Hey!"

Gary Propst, a communications technician in the Canaveral launch room, snapped his head back to his monitor and this time thought he saw what looked like a bright flicker of light in the spacecraft window. Slayton looked at his monitor and saw the same.

White's voice now cut through the crackle in the controllers' headsets. "Fire! We've got a fire in the cockpit!" he shouted.

On the scaffold-like gantry that surrounded the rocket, technician James Gleaves heard the cry and began bounding up the staircase toward the white room. When he burst through the door, he saw flames through the windows, too, and saw that other technicians were already converging on the capsule, trying to open the hatch. Intense heat radiated from the metal hull, forcing them to turn their faces to avoid the full power of it.

"Get them out of there!" shouted Donald Babbitt, the pad leader.

Those men in the white room who were still wearing their headsets could now hear Chaffee shouting, "We have a bad fire!"

They could also hear the incongruously calm voice of Chuck Gay, the test director, who was inside the launch room and had no way of knowing the pandemonium playing out 224 feet aboveground at the tip of the *Saturn* rocket.

"Crew, egress," Gay instructed. "Crew, can you egress at this time?"

Propst, who knew that the crew could very much not egress, now shouted inexplicably, "Blow the hatch! Why don't they blow the hatch?" As if the bank-vault-like door that locked the astronauts inside the *Apollo* could be blown at all.

Some of the members of the pad crew grabbed fire extinguishers, which was what the rules called for but would do no good until the sealed *Apollo* oven in which the fire was roaring could be opened up. Other men continued to try to struggle with the hatch.

Babbitt picked up his emergency phone. "I need firemen, ambulances and equipment," he shouted, and then slammed down the receiver and lunged back toward the hatch to assist with the struggle to open it.

Then, desperately, the voice of Chaffee rang through the headsets on the launchpad, in the launch room and nearly 900 miles away in Houston. What he cried were the words, "We're burning up!"

And so they were. But there was nothing—utterly nothing—that could be done to change that fact now, and as the heat streaming off the spacecraft increased and the men who had been converging on it retreated, one more voice rang out in the room, though no one ever knew whose it was.

"Clear the level!" the person called.

He was using the agreed-upon language to order all of the people outside the ship to back away—or, if possible, to run away—because the spacecraft was in danger of exploding.

Moments later, the *Apollo* gave off a sound and a blast of air like a bomb as it ruptured on its lower right edge, adjacent to Chaffee's seat, showering the white room with flaming debris and setting fire to loose papers on clipboards and desks. Inside the spacecraft, the fire, which had fed on the confined oxygen, rushed toward the freedom of the opening, completely engulfing the astronauts.

Kraft, at his console in Houston, heard every word the dying men said. Slayton—sitting at his console in Florida, not folded up in the equipment bay of the burning ship—heard it all, too, as did every other man in the two control centers. No one, however, would ever be able to agree on exactly what the astronauts' final words were. Even when recordings of the last few seconds of the men's lives were played, different people remembered hearing different things that the tape didn't capture.

What many of the men insisted they did hear was one of the astronauts—a professional pilot to the last, a man who knew that as long as you are able to communicate with your flight controllers you must keep them apprised of the condition of your ship—say as levelly as the circumstances would allow, "I'm reporting a bad fire." That report would be duly noted.

It would be many minutes—far too many minutes—before trucks from the Cape Canaveral fire station at last made it to the launchpad. And it would be many minutes more before the hatch would finally be wrestled open and James Burch, the Cape fire chief, would peer inside. There was not much he could see through the gloaming without a bright flashlight, but when he shined it about he saw the men in a mortal tableau.

All three men were still in their seats, which is where their training would have taught them to be, as they fought to open the hatch and stay in radio communication with the controllers outside. Burch took in the scene for a sorrowful moment and then emerged.

"They are all dead," he said quietly and officially. "The fire is extinguished."

There would be an inquest and a formal investigation and, as one more part of the tragedy, a congressional hearing. Ultimately, the cause of the fire would be traced to a single spark that jumped from a wire on the left side of the cockpit, adjacent to Grissom's seat. The wire ran beneath a little storage compartment with a metal door that had been opened and closed many times without anybody noticing that each time the door moved, it abraded a bit more of the wire's insulation, finally leaving raw, electrically charged copper exposed.

When the wire did spark during the plugs-out test, it ignited a small fire that stayed small only for a second or two. Accelerated by the pure oxygen, the flame climbed along the left-hand wall of the spacecraft, feeding on fabric and netting used for storage. That wall was the worst possible place for a fire to erupt since it prevented Grissom from reaching a latch that would have opened a valve and vented the high-pressure atmosphere, thus slowing the flames.

Unimpeded, the fire proceeded to consume anything around it that would burn—the paper of the flight plans, the cloth of the seats, the Velcro and plastic and rubber that were everywhere. It fed on the space suits of the men themselves, spreading over Grissom and toward White and finally, after the spacecraft ruptured, over Chaffee, too.

The wait would be long, until October of 1968, before a completely redesigned, completely rebuilt *Apollo* would fly. Wally Schirra would command that mission that should have been Grissom's. Seven months later, on July 20, 1969, *Apollo 11* would at last land in the Sea of Tranquility, fulfilling Kennedy's audacious pledge.

The twelve men who walked on the moon would leave plenty of rubbish and hardware and even three lunar rovers behind, a heap of high-tech refuse that may or may not have reflected well on the US space program. But America would leave behind three other things, too. On the far side of the moon, deep in the southern lunar hemisphere, was an isolated basin containing a cluster of three craters—craters that had always been known only by catalogue numbers. They would now be known as Craters Grissom, White and Chaffee.

Those three men—men who'd hoped to fly—were surely lost too soon. The tribute on the moon they had one day hoped to touch would last forever.

This chapter was adapted from the author's previous work in his books Apollo 8: *The Thrilling Story of the First Mission to the Moon* and *To the Moon!: The True Story of the American Heroes on the* Apollo 8 *Spaceship.*

The Soyuz *spacecraft, seen here in a life-size mock-up, has a half-century history of reliability, but its first test flight ended in tragedy.*

❯ FIVE ❯

THE UNLUCKY MISSION OF *SOYUZ 1*

Soyuz 1, 1967

COSMONAUTS AND ASTRONAUTS do not believe in curses. It just isn't in their nature. Curses are things of superstition and magic and strange powers working in mysterious ways. Cosmonauts and astronauts are engineers and pilots who work in the knowable world of physics and equations and tangible machines. No room for magical thinking there.

Still, the time came when they had to wonder if some dark charm had struck them all. That time was 1967, a year that, before it was even half over, seemed to have fallen under a curse. Indeed, the year itself seemed almost to *be* the curse.

At first, 1967 shimmered with promise for both the American and Soviet space programs. The United States in particular had been on an astonishing winning streak for almost two years. From March of 1965 to November of 1966, NASA had been flying its brand-new, souped-up *Gemini* spacecraft, and over the course of that short period had launched and completed ten remarkable missions. American astronauts had learned how to walk in space, to rendezvous and dock in space and to fly up to record-breaking altitudes as high as 850 miles above the Earth.

Yes, there were some problems. Gene Cernan didn't have a whole lot of fun on his Gemini 9 space walk. Neil Armstrong and Dave Scott would probably just as soon forget their near-death experience aboard the out-of-control *Gemini 8*. But everybody came home healthy and whole, and the rough patches and emergencies were all part of the learning process. Now, in November of 1966, the *Gemini* program was done, and in just three months—sometime in mid-February 1967—the three-man *Apollo* spacecraft would begin flying, and it would be the *Apollo*s that would go to the moon.

The Soviets had been having a rougher time of things. Their first generation of spacecraft, the one-person *Vostok*s, had flown six successful missions from 1961 to 1963. But since then, there had been only two other flights. Certainly, those missions were dazzlers: *Voskhod 1*, in 1964, was the first spacecraft to carry a three-person crew, and during *Voskhod 2*, in 1965, a two-cosmonaut mission, Alexei Leonov became the first human being to walk in space.

So confident were the Soviets after those flights that they decided to jump straight ahead to their next generation of spacecraft—the nimble, high-performance *Soyuz* series, which could carry three-person crews and, like the *Apollo*s, were designed for eventual travel to the moon. But tragedy struck in January 1966, when Sergei Korolev, the Soviets' chief rocket engineer, grew ill and died. Korolev was such an extraordinarily great designer, he had actually gone by just that name: the Great Designer. He was replaced by the respected Vasily Mishin, also an extraordinary engineer, though he didn't have Korolev's particular talent for inspiring confidence and respect.

Mishin worked hard, but progress on the *Soyuz* slowed. By early 1967, there had been three unmanned test flights of the new rocket and spacecraft, all of which had failed. Still, as with the *Gemini*s, the Soviets had learned from the setbacks, and as the new year dawned, the glittering new *Soyuz*es—like the glittering new *Apollo*s—were poised to fly.

The grand kickoff for the grand year took place early in the evening on January 27, when astronauts, space officials and dignitaries from the US, the Soviet Union and other countries gathered at the White House in Washington for a cocktail reception to celebrate the signing of a new outer-space treaty. The accord committed spacefaring countries to help rescue one another's crews if they were in trouble and to keep military weapons out of orbit and off the moon or other celestial bodies. Space would be a place of peaceful exploration.

But even as the celebratory event at the White House was coming to an end, the first of those glittering *Apollo*s was bursting into flames on a launchpad at Cape Canaveral during a countdown rehearsal, instantly killing astronauts Gus Grissom, Ed White and Roger Chaffee. By the time the White House guests got to their cars and turned on their radios or returned to their hotel rooms and switched on their TVs, they had heard the news.

The people of NASA, and of America as a whole, were devastated. And the people of the Soviet Union were shocked and deeply saddened, too. The two countries may have been in a footrace to the moon, but they would never want any harm to come to the other side. American and Soviet gymnastics or ice-skating teams might compete ferociously during the Olympics, but no matter who won, they'd still hug at the end of the competition and wish one another safe travels back home. Space was the same way.

The day after the fire, President Johnson received a note from Anatoly Dobrynin, the Soviet ambassador to the United States: "Please, accept, Mr. President, my deepest sympathy in the loss of the three valiant men. The three astronauts, without doubt, could have made a new contribution to the peaceful exploration of the outer space new vistas to which were opened by the Space Treaty signed yesterday."

English, of course, was not Dobrynin's first language. Soviet embassies usually did not allow clumsy phrasing and punctuation in letters to heads of state. But Dobrynin wanted no one cleaning up—and thus scrubbing away his true feelings.

But if the Soviets saw terrible loss in the tragedy that had befallen the Americans, they could not help but see opportunity, too. NASA was facing a long flightless period of its own, perhaps as long as the Soviets' recent two years, as they redesigned their firetrap *Apollo*. That left the skies to the *Soyuz*—and the plans were ambitious ones.

Sometime in the spring—no later than April—*Soyuz 1* would go aloft with just one cosmonaut in a ship that could accommodate three. The next day, *Soyuz 2*, with a full three-person crew, would follow. The two spacecraft would rendezvous and dock in space—a delicate maneuver the Americans had achieved but the Soviets hadn't yet. Then two of the crew members from *Soyuz 2* would exit their ship, spacewalk over to *Soyuz 1* and climb inside. *Soyuz 1* would then come home with three cosmonauts and *Soyuz 2* with just one. Over the course of only a few days, the Soviets would match nearly all of the feats it had taken the Americans ten *Gemini* missions to accomplish. Just like that, the space race would be a dead heat again.

The question for the Soviets was which cosmonauts would get the nod to make the historic flights and who, in particular, would be the one to go first and alone aboard *Soyuz 1*. The answer was actually easy.

Yuri Gagarin was the most celebrated cosmonaut in Soviet history and, as the first human being in space, an icon around the world as well. His face was on postage stamps, wall mosaics and tribute coins all over the Soviet Union, but the secret was, he would never fly again. The Soviets dared not risk the life of so important a man by putting him back on top of a giant rocket filled with explosive fuel and lighting the fuse. Gagarin would continue to be part of the cosmonaut corps, but even for as important a mission as Soyuz 1, which would have benefited from his piloting talents, he would never actually be chosen to fly.

The mission instead went to Gagarin's close friend Vladimir Komarov—and that was a good choice. At forty, Komarov was older than nearly all of the other cosmonauts, but he had made very good use of his years. During World War II, when he was just fifteen, he enlisted in the Soviet air force school, earning his wings just as the war ended. While serving in the air force, he applied to be a cosmonaut and was quickly accepted. Two brushes with poor health—a hernia operation and a suspicious flutter in his heartbeat—kept him grounded, but Komarov persisted. His wife, Valentina, encouraged him, and he promised his young son, Yevgeny, and his younger daughter, Irina, that one day they would see their hero father fly in space.

And they did. In 1964, Komarov commanded the three-man crew of *Voskhod 1*, distinguishing himself not only as a talented, coolheaded cosmonaut, but as a natural leader as well. *Soyuz 1* called for both of those skills. Yevgeny, now sixteen, and Irina, now nine, would see their father become the first cosmonaut to fly in space twice.

What the children—and their mother and the rest of the Soviet Union—could not know was that there were a lot of reasons to wonder whether Komarov should go at all. Those three failed unmanned flights of the *Soyuz* rocket and spacecraft were on a lot of people's minds, though the Russian engineers promised they'd worked out the causes of the glitches.

More troubling was the fact that those same engineers, along with the cosmonauts, had recently compiled a list of more than 200 engineering problems that still plagued the spacecraft. Everyone involved could have benefited from a few extra weeks, or even months, to keep working on the problems and get them solved, but there was another matter to consider. May Day was approaching—the May 1 holiday that in the Soviet Union was a little like a combination of America's Labor Day and the Fourth of July. And 1967 was the fiftieth anniversary of the start of the Russian Revolution—as important to the Soviets as the American Revolution is to Americans. The Soviet government very much wanted a great space triumph to mark the upcoming celebration, and the pressure was on to get *Soyuz 1* and *2* off the pad and into space before May 1 arrived.

So the decision was made. On April 13, eight cosmonauts, the four who were the prime crews of *Soyuz 1* and *2* and the four who were the backup crews, flew to the Baikonur Cosmodrome in Kazakhstan—the Soviet Union's Cape Canaveral. There, they took up residence in the comfortable cottages where crews would share their meals and have their meetings and bunk down at night as they prepared for the grand adventure that was approaching.

The launch dates were set for April 23 for *Soyuz 1* and April 24 for *Soyuz 2*, and for all of the problems the *Soyuz* had had getting itself flight ready, the first launch went precisely as it was supposed to. Liftoff was scheduled for 6:35 a.m. in Baikonur—still dark and always cold at that hour in that month on the Kazakh steppe. Komarov went to bed late in the afternoon the day before—around 5:30 p.m.—was allowed six hours of sleep and was then awakened at 11:30 p.m. He ate a midnight breakfast, underwent a medical check and, with the help of technicians, climbed into his space suit. Gagarin assisted him, too, and in fact never left his side. About three hours before launch, they climbed into a van and were driven to the launchpad.

Six years before, in 1961, Gagarin had made that same

ride out to the same pad, on his way to making history. Either because he had had too much coffee and juice at breakfast or because he was nervous, or both, the man, who in a few hours would be a legend, realized that he very much had to pee. His flight would be short—just eighty-eight minutes—but he would be lying on his back in his spacecraft for hours before he launched. So Gagarin asked the driver to pull over, hopped out of the van, unfastened his space suit and, right there on the chilly steppe, peed against the tire of the van. Gagarin's flight went perfectly, and even engineer pilots knew a lucky charm when they saw one. So every single one of them decided that forevermore, space crews heading to the pad would always stop on the way for a bit of personal relief, including using the van tire as a target, just like Gagarin had. Komarov honored the tradition, too.

Finally, out at the launchpad, he and Gagarin climbed into the cage-like elevator next to the rocket, rode the 150 feet up to the top, and with the assistance of more technicians, Komarov was helped into the center seat. The seats to the right and left of him would remain empty until, two days later, high above in orbit, the *Soyuz 2* cosmonauts joined him.

Gagarin returned to the ground and hurried back to the control center, where he would be one of the spacecraft communicators, in constant contact with his friend in space. On the ground, Gagarin might call Komarov by his first name, Vladimir, but when he called the ship, he would address him as *Rubin*, Russian for ruby—the code name for *Soyuz 1*.

Precisely on time, at 6:35 a.m., the twenty engines on the

bottom of the rocket 150 feet below *Rubin* ignited, turning the darkened steppe to brilliant day, and the first *Soyuz* spacecraft to carry a human being climbed into the sky. Just over eleven minutes later, that human being and his spacecraft were orbiting more than 122 miles above the Earth.

Straightaway, the problems began. The *Soyuz* was designed with two wings that would unfold and extend from each side once it reached space. Wings, of course, are not necessary to stay aloft in space, where there is no air and where the physics of velocity and gravity are all that is required to keep a spacecraft circling the Earth. But wings are vital when they're covered with solar cells that absorb the energy from the sun and convert it into electricity. *Soyuz 1*'s wings would provide Komarov nearly all of the power he needed—or at least they were supposed to. Except that only one of them unfolded. The other one, no matter how many times Komarov flipped the switch that was supposed to extend it—and no matter how many times the ground sent up a similar command—remained folded and closed.

Throughout the first of his ninety-minute orbits, Komarov tried to position his spacecraft so that the one open panel would collect as much light as possible, but that proved difficult, as the constantly moving *Soyuz* forever changed its position relative to the sun. He tried throughout the second orbit, too, but he still had little luck, and the one working panel spent a great deal of time completely in shadow. That meant it was providing no power at all, and Komarov was running on batteries, which could only last so long.

"The current of the solar panel is zero," he reported.

The downlink was poor, and the controllers didn't hear him well, so they asked him to repeat. The exasperated cosmonaut obliged them.

"Zero, zero! There's nothing. A zero, a zero!"

That time the controllers could not mistake his meaning. And there was worse to report as the day continued. The spacecraft had two automatic systems to help it maintain the proper orientation, so that it could point its nose in just the right direction for the rendezvous with *Soyuz 2* that was supposed to happen the next day, as well as for the burn of the engine that would ease the ship out of orbit and bring it home the day after. One of these systems steered the way the ancient sailors had—using the stars as landmarks—while the other used much newer technology, but neither one was working properly. What's more, two of the spacecraft's thrusters—the little jets that moved the ship to the position the orientation systems were supposed to tell it to point—were losing fuel pressure.

All of these together led the ground controllers to a painful conclusion: launching *Soyuz 2* would be a waste of time. You could hardly execute a delicate dance like a meet-up and docking in space if one of the ships could barely hold itself straight. The only thing to do now was to keep the increasingly broken-down *Soyuz 1* functioning just long enough to get its one crew member home safely. That also demanded that he come home soon, before even more could go wrong—immediately, if possible. But the fact was, it *wasn't* possible.

Orbiting spacecraft can't return from space any time at

all; they have to wait for just the right moment in just the right orbit so that the trajectory—or the path the ship follows as it descends—will bring it back to the proper recovery site, which in this case would be in the same open plains of Kazakhstan, not far from the city of Karaganda. By now, Komarov had been in space for about fifteen orbits, or just over twenty-two hours, and to hit the proper target, he'd have to wait three more hours before he could head home. Mishin called the ship to give him the news.

"Rubin, respond please," Mishin said.

"I hear you," Komarov answered.

"Rubin, I am asking you to rest and get ready for landing on the seventeenth orbit. How do you read me?"

Komarov read Mishin just fine. And Komarov read the meaning of that command, too. His spacecraft had failed, and even if that wasn't his fault, his mission had also failed. There would be no joint flight with his friends on the ground. No docking. No historic space walk and crew exchange. The Soviets would not match the remarkable things the Americans had done in the last two years, at least not yet. And Komarov, who loved his country as much as the Americans loved their own, would not be able to give it the wonderful May Day present he'd imagined. But if all of that went through his head, he betrayed none of it.

"I read you," he said. "At the current time, I can rest and get ready for landing on the seventeenth."

When the seventeenth orbit at last began, Komarov buckled his seat restraints and prepared, as ordered, to come home, a maneuver that would be trickier than it typically was. With the two automatic orientation systems not functioning, he would have to use his hand controllers to fire his thrusters and position the ship manually. He still had one exceedingly well-functioning guidance and orientation system—his eyes—and that system would have to be sufficient.

Komarov's spacecraft slowly approached the precise spot in the orbit that would allow him to come down where the recovery teams would be waiting. He watched his countdown clock, reviewed the reentry procedures in his head and then began to fire his thrusters, positioning the ship just so. On the ground, Gagarin was on the microphone, with other members of the flight team nearby.

"With me here are a lot of friends who are sending warm greetings, the kindest wishes for a soft, good landing," he said. "Best of luck. We're waiting on Earth."

"Thanks for your wishes," Komarov answered. "Not much time before we meet, so I'll see you soon. Wish you success in everything."

"Thank you, friend. We're waiting here; we're waiting impatiently."

Komarov then fired his engines and let them burn for the precise two minutes and twenty-six seconds that would be needed for the ship to surrender to Earth's gravity. Then he shut them off and was on his way home.

As distant as space can be, it doesn't take long to return from Earth orbit—a twenty-minute plunge through the atmosphere and you're home. But that plunge isn't easy. A reentering *Soyuz* spacecraft would normally descend a little like a roller coaster, following a rising and falling path that would allow it to bleed off speed gradually. A ride like that would still be awfully rough, subjecting the cosmonaut to a force of four times the Earth's gravity—or four g's. If Komarov weighed 150 pounds, he'd feel like he weighed 600 pounds, and all of that weight would seem to be pressed across his chest, making it hard to breathe.

That kind of reentry would be uncomfortable enough, but in the case of an emergency like Komarov's, the ground controllers could not trust a malfunctioning spacecraft to execute all the necessary climbs and dips properly. Instead, the ship would be sent on what amounted to a straight plunge, called a ballistic reentry. It was simpler and more reliable, but it also meant doubling the four g's to a crushing load of eight g's. Komarov would now feel like he weighed 1,200 pounds.

Still, cosmonauts had trained for even more than that, and Komarov, a veteran of one space flight already, was especially well prepared. Just to be sure, though, the ground radioed up to him to make sure all was well.

"How do you feel; how are you? Over," one of the controllers asked.

"I feel excellent," Komarov said. "Everything is in order."

"Understood," the controller responded. "Here, comrades are recommending for you to take deep breaths. We're waiting for the landing."

"Thank you to everyone," Komarov said.

At that moment, Komarov heard a small bang and felt a bump, but even in his malfunctioning spacecraft, that was a good thing. The reentry engines were located in a separate section of the *Soyuz*, attached to its bottom by bolts filled with tiny explosive charges. Now that the engines were no longer needed, the bolts would blow, causing the entire engine section to fall away, and exposing a sturdy heat shield that would protect the remaining part of the *Soyuz* from the high temperatures, exceeding 3,000 degrees, that are generated by friction as the spacecraft falls through the thickening air.

"Separation," Komarov called to the ground.

"Rubin, understood," the ground controller said. "Separation occurred."

If Komarov said anything else, no one heard him because at that moment, all communications with the ship were suddenly lost. That was to be expected, too. The heat of the reentry was by now causing charged gas known as plasma to form around the spacecraft, trailing it like a comet's tail. The plasma, in turn, would disrupt radio communications with the ship. The blackout would last a few minutes, and by the time it was over, the worst part of the reentry would be over, too. When Komarov emerged from the radio silence, his parachutes would have popped open and he'd be on his way to a safe landing. The next time the controllers heard his voice, they'd know all was well and he was truly coming home.

After those few minutes had elapsed, the ground controller again called the ship. There was no answer, but by this point that did not necessarily mean a problem. So much on *Soyuz 1* had broken down already, it seemed almost inevitable that the communications system would fail, too.

Out in the vast fields in Kazakhstan where the spacecraft was supposed to land, the news was better. One of the spotters in one of the search-and-rescue helicopters converging on the scene reported that he could see the spacecraft descending. The others saw it, too, and all of them closed in. It was just like the problem-plagued *Soyuz 1* to have radio issues that would make it impossible for its crew to communicate even after the ship was through the plasma blackout. But that kind of malfunction was precisely the reason the spotters were dispatched in the first place, and today they had done their jobs. From now on, they would have no problem keeping track of the ship. It was spring, and the fields were green and grassy, which would make it easy to spot the dark, slightly charred *Soyuz* once it thumped down. Its orange-and-white parachute, spread across the field, should be even easier to pick out.

Moments later, exactly as the rescuers had hoped, they saw what they were looking for. The spacecraft was on the ground, the chute was nearby, and Komarov, to their great relief, was back on Earth. The helicopters raced in to the spot, but even as they were approaching, they could see that something was wrong. The parachutes looked crumpled. The ship looked blacker than it should. The moment the helicopters touched down, the rescuers hopped out and began sprinting toward the *Soyuz*. Before they could reach it, a great blast of fire burst from its bottom.

That blast, the rescuers knew, was caused by braking rockets that were supposed to have lit just a second or so before the spacecraft touched the ground, helping to cushion the final bump.

If it happened now, well after the landing, it meant something was very wrong. The spacecraft, they could now also see, was lying on its side.

Worse, it was suddenly impossible to get anywhere near the ship. The braking rockets had ignited a terrible fire, generating a ferocious heat. Oily black clouds of smoke were swirling from the spacecraft; melted metal was dripping onto the ground.

One of the rescuers flipped on his radio and shouted into it, "The cosmonaut needs urgent medical attention out in the field!"

It would soon become clear, though, that the cosmonaut was beyond the help of any such attention. As the rescuers fought through the flames with fire extinguishers, they could see that the spacecraft was badly misshapen, even flattened, as if it had not slowly descended from the sky during the final minutes of its return under the care of a parachute, but instead had plummeted straight from space. The tangled chute lying uselessly nearby confirmed that suspicion. Even if the fall had not killed Komarov, the heat of his burning ship would have. No human could survive that fire and violence. The commander of *Soyuz 1* was surely dead.

A later investigation would determine that the parachute system was indeed to blame for the tragedy. The *Soyuz* had two main chutes: one that was supposed to do the job of bringing the ship home safely, and one that would immediately take over if that first one did not deploy properly. But on this most unlucky spacecraft, both chutes failed, and Komarov had slammed into the hard ground at nearly 124 miles per hour.

The loss of Vladimir Komarov, the first human being to die during a space flight, was announced at 5:30 p.m. in the Soviet Union. The official government press statement was somber and simple: "The untimely death of the outstanding spaceman test-engineer of spaceships Vladimir Mikhaylovich Komarov is a great loss for the whole Soviet people." Many of those Soviet people responded by pouring into Red Square, the huge, ceremonial center of Moscow. There, as they listened to the news on radios, many of them embraced and just as many cried—all of them standing in the square under the rain that was beginning to fall over the city.

Even before the news was broken to the Soviet Union at large, it was broken in a much more private way to a much smaller group. On the outskirts of Moscow, a black car carrying a government official pulled up to the modest home where the Komarov family lived. Out here in the suburbs, the rain was falling much harder. That—the cold downpour as the stranger knocked on the door—was the detail Komarov's daughter, Irina, would always remember when she thought about that night. Her mother knew—as the wives of all astronauts and cosmonauts and test pilots knew when a man in a black car appeared at the door— that there was only one reason he would be there. He told her his news anyway. She asked him if he was certain, and he told her sorrowfully that he was.

Komarov's remains were cremated and then interred in the Kremlin wall, at the edge of Red Square, where other heroes of the Soviet Union rest. Later, a memorial was constructed at the precise spot his ship had hit the ground, in the then-green field in Kazakhstan. A year later, the Soviet Union would suffer again, when Komarov's friend Gagarin would join him in the Kremlin wall, having died in a plane crash during a training run. The nation grieved again and the families wept again. But there was solace in the knowledge that Gagarin and Komarov, friends who had worked together and trained together, would now rest forever together.

The upper stage of the lunar module Snoopy, *as it approached the mother ship* Charlie Brown. *By the time this picture was taken,* Apollo 10's *Tom Stafford and Gene Cernan had survived their near-disaster above the moon.*

> SIX >

THE TUMBLING MOONSHIP

Apollo 10, 1969

THERE WERE A lot of mission rules in the official flight plan when *Apollo 10* was preparing to leave Earth on its journey to the moon, but the most important one was: whatever you do, don't land there. Landing on the moon may have been why the astronauts signed up to fly in space in the first place, but for Apollo 10, the space agency bosses were clear all the same: touch the moon and you're in deep trouble. That was not an easy order for the three men of Apollo 10 to obey.

They had an *Apollo* spacecraft—a command-service module that was perfectly capable of going into orbit around the moon. And they had an attached lunar excursion module— or LEM—the buggy four-legged ship designed to get two of the three astronauts down from lunar orbit, onto the surface of the moon and back up to orbit again.

The Apollo 9 boys had had a LEM and a command module,

too, but they had flown only around the Earth, taking the fragile, foil-covered lander on its first shakedown cruise in space.

Apollo 8 actually did fly to the moon, but that crew didn't have a lander at all. Yes, they had made history as the first human beings to orbit the moon and see its far side; still, while they had traveled more than 233,000 miles to enter that orbit, they had no way to close the final sixty miles and land.

Now, on the morning of May 18, 1969, *Apollo 10* was poised on the launchpad, its 363-foot *Saturn V* rocket outgassing liquid oxygen plumes into the Cape Canaveral sky, its command module perched on top and a perfectly functional, perfectly beautiful lunar module packed inside the rocket's upper stage, ready to fly from Florida to the moon.

And yet there was the no-landing rule.

NASA had its reasons for that, and they were pretty good ones. The LEM had been an incorrigibly difficult machine to design and build. It was chronically behind schedule, overweight and underachieving, with its computer, its guidance hardware, its life-support systems and more causing no end of headaches.

The *Apollo 9* flight in Earth orbit had been fine, but lunar orbit was a different thing altogether. The moon's lumpy sub-surface meant an equally lumpy gravity field that could cause unpredictable wobbles in the ship's trajectory. The landing techniques had been developed but not rehearsed. The radar and navigation systems had similarly not been tried anywhere near the lunar vicinity.

If any of those variables or a thousand more went bad, the two men who tried to fly down to the lunar surface might never get back, getting stranded on the ground if they didn't crash into it first, and leaving the one crew member who had remained in lunar orbit to fly home alone. NASA wanted no part of the globally televised spectacle of packing three men into a spacecraft, sending them out to the moon and getting just one of them back after splashdown.

The *Apollo 10* astronauts had made peace with their limited mission, which is what would be expected from three such experienced pilots. Tom Stafford, the commander; John Young, the command module pilot; and Gene Cernan, the lunar module pilot, had five flights among them already and understood NASA's stepwise ways of doing things.

What's more, even without a landing, their flight would be plenty adventurous. Stafford and Cernan would fly the LEM down from the sixty-mile altitude at which both ships orbited to just 9.4 miles above the lunar surface, or about the altitude military aircraft fly over the Earth. That was stunt flying of the first order, and they were itching to do it.

And if the 9.4 miles they would not cover were all that would deny Stafford his chance to be the first man on the moon, Cernan his chance to be the second and Young his chance to be part of the most epic journey in human history, well, the astronauts would just have to make peace with that.

What the *Apollo 10* crew didn't know—couldn't know—was that just over four days after launch, Stafford and Cernan would be a lot closer to closing those 9.4 miles and reaching the lunar surface than they planned to be. Their route there, however, would not be the steady powered descent of a controlled lunar landing but a violent, tumbling plunge, one that would threaten to take the lives of both men while Young orbited overhead, powerless to help them.

If Apollo 10 was serious business, it was also going to be a lot of fun, and the crew had made it clear they were going to keep things light.

The *Apollo 9* astronauts had given their twin spacecraft call signs: the cone-shaped command module would be Gumdrop and the insect-like LEM would be Spider. Already, word was going around that NASA expected something more dignified for the lunar landing missions—names like Eagle and Columbia or Yankee Clipper and Intrepid.

But Apollo 10 would not be a landing, so like the astronauts of *Apollo 9*, the men could take their inspiration from wherever they wanted, and they took it from the *Peanuts* cartoon. The command module would be dubbed *Charlie Brown* and the lunar module would be *Snoopy*, and if anyone wanted to complain about that, they were welcome to risk their own necks flying the two machines. No one did complain.

The mission's fun began the moment the *Saturn V* rocket lifted off.

"What a ride, babe, what a ride!" Cernan called as soon as the giant machine left the ground. *Babe* was easily Cernan's favorite nickname, a term of affection he applied to women, men, children and even airplanes and rockets if they pleased him.

"Just like old times! It's beautiful out there!" said Young when the crew reached space just seventeen minutes later.

"You guys sound ecstatic," said the capcom, calling up from Houston.

"Man, this is the greatest!" Stafford confirmed.

It would remain the greatest, too, at least for a while. *Apollo 8*'s translunar trip had taken place five months ago, and the world had sweated every mile of it. But with one lunar journey in the books, everyone relaxed a little.

The *Apollo 10* crew beamed color TV broadcasts back to Earth—so much crisper and prettier than the black-and-white images from *Apollo 8*'s trip. At a distance of 129,000 miles, halfway to the moon, the astronauts captured a view of the home planet and sent it to the 3.5 billion other people living there—a blue-white sphere hanging in space, with the North American continent clearly visible.

"I'm voting for the world being round," Cernan said.

Stafford swung the camera around to show Young inside the cockpit, displaying a drawing of *Charlie Brown* and then one of *Snoopy*, after which the crew played a recording of the song "Fly Me to the Moon" from a small tape recorder they had packed along for the ride.

Thirty-six hours and another hundred thousand miles later, things got more serious. As the command module and the lunar module, linked end to end, entered the lunar neighborhood, the moon's gravity would take hold of the twinned ships and swing them around its far side. If the astronauts did nothing, they would simply whip around the near side and get flung home like a stone from a slingshot.

To go into orbit instead, they would have to approach

the moon backward with their engine bell pointed forward. The maneuver, called the lunar orbit insertion, or LOI, would require them to fire the engine for four minutes to slow down just enough to surrender to the moon's gravity and go into orbit. If they burned too long, they'd slow down so much that the intended orbit would collapse and they'd plummet to the moon's surface.

Two things would make the maneuver harder still. The navigation computer required the engine burn to be conducted when the spacecraft was situated in such a way that its windows pointed up, meaning that the astronauts wouldn't be able to see the moon while they were executing the critical burn.

What's more, since they would be behind the moon when they lit the engine, they'd also be out of contact with Houston until they appeared around the front again. The burn would be conducted both in the blind and in radio blackout.

When the craft at last disappeared behind the back of the moon, the *Apollo 10* astronauts, like no one in history save the *Apollo 8* crew before them, were beings wholly disconnected from the rest of humanity. They could look up into the blackness of space; they could take it as an article of faith that the great bulk of the moon was just below them, but apart from that, they were entirely cut off.

"We're on our own now," Stafford said in a moment of uncharacteristic reflectiveness. He craned his neck toward his window, looking for the moon, which he knew was impossible to see. A bit of the LEM, which was attached to the nose of his ship, was all that was visible.

"Don't see anything?" Cernan asked.

"No, and I don't care to see anything now," Stafford said, shaking off his brief reverie and turning his attention back to his instruments.

Cernan began to look toward his instruments, too, but then did see something. It was a faint brightening in the spacecraft, as a light of some kind began to stream into the window. He looked up and saw nothing and then all at once did—it was the moon, below them, reflecting off of *Snoopy*'s windows and pouring its light into *Charlie Brown*'s.

"I got the moon's surface!" he exclaimed. "I can see it in the window!"

"Good show!" Stafford answered.

"It's down there, babe! It's beautiful! We're right on top of it," Cernan said.

Young, who had no patience for such foolishness, not with the engine burn only minutes away, answered both of his crewmates in the best way he could.

"Translational control power is armed," he said, reading from the flight plan.

The other two men collected themselves, followed Young's lead and got back to business. Six minutes later, they lit their engine. Four minutes after that, they shut it off, and with that became satellites of another world.

"We is at the moon, fellows!" Cernan said. "Can you believe it?"

"It's fascinating," Young conceded.

"Well, what do we do now?" Cernan asked with a laugh.

Then, with a wink at Young, he answered his own question. "Read the flight plan, I guess," he said.

That flight plan, as the astronauts knew, called for some tough and fancy flying. Just over a day after arriving in orbit, Stafford and Cernan would crawl through the tunnel that connected the lunar module and the command-service module, shut the hatch and cast off.

From a high of sixty miles, they would burn *Snoopy*'s engine in the same kind of braking maneuver *Charlie Brown* had used to enter lunar orbit, this time to bleed off enough speed to descend to the appointed 9.4-mile altitude—a critical point because it was close to there that the next crew would begin their final descent to landing.

For this mission, though, with no landing planned, they would then relight their engine, fly back up to sixty miles, relink with the command module and climb back aboard.

Making things more challenging was that the LEM was actually a two-part spacecraft. Its bottom half, the part with the legs, was known as the descent module, and its job, as its name suggested, was to fire its engine and get the astronauts down to the surface of the moon. From that point on, the descent module's job was mostly done, save to serve as a launch platform for the ascent stage—the upper half of the spacecraft. When the time came to leave the moon, explosive bolts would separate the two stages, and the ascent stage, with the two astronauts aboard, would light its own engine and fly back to orbit to link up with the mother ship, while the descent stage would be left on the moon.

The *Apollo 10* astronauts would practice that separation and ignition maneuver from their 9.4-mile altitude. That would be a good test of the ascent engine, and it would also be a chance to rehearse the emergency abort procedures that would be used on any lunar landing trip in the event that a future crew got partway down and then had to break off the landing and hightail it back to the mother ship. For that reason, the *Apollo 10* maneuver would be run by the computer program known as the abort guidance system, or AGS.

All that was for later, though. First, the astronauts would have to separate the two ships, leaving Young alone in *Charlie Brown*. The entire maneuver would be beamed back to Mission Control and televisions across America, courtesy of the same color TV camera the crew had used for the more casual broadcast earlier.

"*Snoopy* and *Charlie Brown*, we see you separating on the big tube," said the capcom in Houston.

"Have a good time while we're gone, babe," Cernan called to Young.

"Don't get lonesome, John," said Stafford.

Over the course of the next four hours, both spacecraft completed two more orbits of the moon, with *Snoopy* moving steadily lower and its reflective, gold-colored shape dwindling from a twenty-three-foot-tall mass of machinery to a tiny gold dot far, far below *Charlie Brown*.

"Boy, are they down among 'em!" marveled Young to Houston.

They were indeed—drawing closer and closer to the jagged peaks of the moon as they prepared to execute their separation and burn.

Cernan's job in the final minutes before the explosive separation of the two halves of the LEM and the ignition of the ascent engine would be to make sure the digital autopilot, or DAP, was configured properly. It was an important part of the AGS, and helped make sure that the computer took into account that the moment the separation occurred, the LEM would have lost about half of its original mass and would have to fly with that lighter weight in mind.

Stafford would then fire the bolts and blow off the descent stage, and Cernan would engage the thrusters and move backward and away from the spent half of the vehicle.

"The DAP is set for a light vehicle," Cernan confirmed to Stafford.

"Okay, okay," Stafford answered. "Thrust aft and hold it. Okay, ready?"

"Okay," Cernan said.

Then Stafford hit his staging switch, a thump and a bang shook the spacecraft and the descent stage was jettisoned. Immediately, that now-useless half of the LEM did precisely what it was supposed to do, which was to begin to drift away from the ascent stage.

Cernan prepared to fire his thrusters to increase that distance, but at that moment, the ascent stage did precisely the kind of thing it wasn't supposed to do, which was to go suddenly, utterly mad. No sooner had it been freed from the descent stage than it began a violent, out-of-control tumble, barrel-rolling through the lunar sky.

Stafford lunged for his thruster handle and Cernan glanced out his window. The lunar horizon was spinning by wildly outside.

"Son of a bitch!" he exclaimed.

On the ground, the men in Mission Control heard the exclamation and sat upright, but said nothing so as not to distract the astronauts. Stafford looked toward the instrument panel and saw the guidance compass spinning as wildly as the ship. A yellow warning light flashed on, indicating that the gyroscopes were about to go into what was called gimbal lock, a condition that would erase their memory entirely and make it impossible to regain control of the ship.

"We're in trouble," Stafford said to Cernan.

"*Snoopy*, Houston, we show you close to gimbal lock," the capcom now radioed up.

Stafford glanced down, saw the warning light again and swung the still-tumbling ship hard around, sweeping the gyros past their lock position.

"We got out of it," he said.

The LEM, however, was still in its spin, and the lunar surface—already dangerously close—continued to reach up to the ship. As Stafford fought with his thrusters, Cernan checked the rate of spin and saw it approaching one revolution per second. That, as any pilot knew, was the rate at which vertigo would set in and the astronauts would begin to suffer tunnel vision and could then lose consciousness. The *Gemini 8* crew had faced exactly this danger when their spacecraft spun out of control, but the danger was even worse in a LEM that was flying so low.

"Gotta get this damn thing . . . ," Cernan muttered. His words poured into his open mic and from there to Mission Control and the world following the unfolding crisis on television.

Stafford continued to battle with his thrusters while Cernan searched for the source of the problem in his digital autopilot and AGS settings.

Seconds of silence passed as Stafford played his sixteen maneuvering jets, thrusting the ship one way, counterthrusting to damp that motion and gradually bringing his out-of-control spacecraft to heel. At last it slowed and stabilized.

"That was something we've never seen before," the relieved commander said to the ground. "But we're all set; we didn't lock it."

John Young, in his higher orbit, just emerging from his behind-the-moon blackout, called to check in. "How was the staging?" he asked Houston.

"*Charlie Brown*," Houston answered, "they got staging. They had a wild gyration, though, but they got it under control."

"I'll tell you, there was a minute there . . . ," Cernan began, and then stopped.

Whatever he was about to observe, it was the kind of thing that gets said when a danger has completely passed and you're free to remark on what a fix you'd been in. But the danger had not passed—not yet. The engine burn that would be needed to get *Snoopy* back up to *Charlie Brown*'s sixty-mile orbit was just five minutes away, and getting past one crisis was no guarantee Stafford and Cernan wouldn't run straight into the next one.

"Houston, I'm not reading them," radioed Young, whose communications link had gone spotty again. "So if they don't make it, you've got to tell me, okay?"

Ultimately, they did make it. The engine burn was a success, the ascent stage with its two-man crew soared back up to its rendezvous altitude, the two ships docked and Stafford and Cernan crawled back through the tunnel into *Charlie Brown*. Once all three men were secure, the remaining half of *Snoopy* was released into space and the *Apollo 10* crew peeled off for home.

Less than three days later, they splashed down in the South Pacific, and just two months after that, *Apollo 11* flew to the moon and closed that final 9.4 miles.

Apollo 10's near-disaster was eventually traced to mere human error. One of the two astronauts in the LEM had engaged the abort guidance system as required by the separation maneuver. The other one, not knowing that that had been done, threw the switch the other way—thinking he was engaging the AGS but actually disengaging it. At the moment of separation, *Snoopy* thus had no idea where it was, and began spinning itself about, trying to spot *Charlie Brown* with its guidance radar. It was precisely the kind of small flaw in a flight plan that rehearsal missions like Apollo 10 were flown to uncover, and in the future, the switch over to AGS would be announced out loud and confirmed out loud.

Today, the *Charlie Brown* command module is on display in the Science Museum of London.

And as for *Snoopy*? *Snoopy* flies on.

On all of the lunar landing missions that followed, the spent ascent modules of the LEMs were deliberately sent on a crash-landing dive into the moon's surface as a first test of the seismometers—which were designed to detect moonquakes—that the crews left there during their moonwalks.

But *Apollo 10* didn't land and could thus leave no seismometer. So Houston radioed *Snoopy* a command to light its engine one last time and fly into a permanent orbit around the sun, so it would not present a danger to future astronauts who would pass this way. Amateur astronomers search for it still, speaking fondly of the old relic as *Apollo*'s lost dog. If it is ever found, it will be observed from afar but never touched, left to continue the long, long journey it began more than two generations ago.

Apollo 12 *lifted off into what, in this picture, appears to be a clear sky. It wasn't, and barely a second later, the* Saturn V *rocket was struck by lightning.*

> SEVEN >

THE MOON TRIP AND THE LIGHTNING STRIKE

Apollo 12, 1969

PETE CONRAD HAD no business trying to fly to the moon on a rainy morning in November of 1969. And NASA, by the look of things, had no business agreeing that it would be a good idea to send him there. You wouldn't know that, however, from the scene at Cape Canaveral.

The *Saturn V* moon rocket was poised on the launchpad, impossible to miss even three miles away—a spike of white, thirty-six stories tall, weighing six and a half million pounds. Five and a half million of those pounds were explosive kerosene, liquid hydrogen and liquid oxygen fuel. Vapor was subliming from the rocket's sides—a bright white against the gray of the sky.

The usual hundreds of thousands of people had lined the beaches in their campers and tents, arriving days before the launch to secure a good spot from which to watch the great rocket fly. The hundreds of dignitaries had assembled in the

VIP stands, a crowd which, that morning, included the newly inaugurated president, Richard Nixon. Less than a year into his first term, Nixon was determined to run an optimistic, open administration, and what better way to demonstrate that than to show the presidential colors at the start of the country's latest moon adventure?

Conrad, the commander of the mission, and his crewmates, Dick Gordon and Al Bean, had already made their ceremonial preflight appearance, sealed in their space suits and grinning through their bubble helmets, as they took the short walk from the suit-up building to the waiting van for the long ride to the pad. Out of the view of the press and public, they had taken the 360-foot elevator ride to the top of the rocket and climbed inside their conical command module.

It was all as orderly and deliberate as the Apollo missions that flew before had been, and there was no reason this one shouldn't get off the ground as uneventfully.

And yet there was the business with the weather.

The cloud ceiling was hanging at just 1,000 feet—an altitude that was technically within limits, even if it was menacingly low.

The wind was blowing at less than twenty miles per hour, which was also within limits—just barely.

There was, happily, no lightning anywhere within a nineteen-mile footprint of the launchpad, which was perhaps the most important consideration of all. But lightning can be fast and it can be fickle and, traveling at the electromagnetic speed it does, it can cover nineteen miles awfully quickly.

The rain, at least, was only intermittent. Still, it was heavy enough when it did fall that it had managed to leak through what was known as the spacecraft's boost protective cover, the formfitting metal shell that covered the *Apollo* capsule at the top of the rocket and would be jettisoned three minutes after launch. Cockpit windows that in a few days would be used for taking sightings of the moon were now beaded with very Earthly rain.

Still, the NASA meteorologists gave the mission a cautious go, and five minutes before launch, the pad controller radioed the cockpit, wishing Conrad and his crew a good trip.

Gordon answered, "Hold off the weather for five more, will you?"

Conrad, a naval aviator and test pilot, had no such worries. "The navy is always glad to do the all-weather testing," he said.

If Conrad was as glad as he said to be going to the moon today, it wasn't necessarily the way he'd imagined going—and the rain wasn't the issue. The issue instead was the mission's numeral: 12—as in Apollo 12.

At the beginning of the year, NASA had announced that *Apollos 9* and *10* would be used as shakedown cruises for both the *Apollo* command module, which was the orbiter and mother ship, and the spidery lunar module. If those missions succeeded, *Apollo 11* would try for the first lunar landing—which meant that Neil Armstrong would be the first man on the moon.

If Neil and his boys didn't make it, the opportunity for the great lunar laurel would go to Conrad, as commander of *Apollo 12*. If he failed, it would be Jim Lovell on *Apollo 13* or Al

Shepard on *14* or Dave Scott on *15*, and on and on until some-body finally stuck the landing.

But Neil, with his famously level head and steady hand, got the job done on the very first try, so the Sea of Tranquility and his remark—"One small step for man, one giant leap for mankind"—became the stuff of historical legend.

Now, four months later, came Conrad, with his planned landing in the Ocean of Storms—and his first words, which far fewer people would pay attention to, because nobody was ever going to ask what the second man to command a spacecraft landing on the moon said when he stepped outside.

All the same, there were compensations to being number two. Armstrong and his lunar module copilot, Buzz Aldrin, spent less than twenty-two hours on the surface of the moon and were outside walking around for barely two and a half of those hours. Conrad and Bean would spend thirty-two hours on the moon and would go outside twice, for a total of about eight hours.

What's more, they'd have a color television camera instead of *Apollo 11*'s flickery black and white, which meant a much better historical record of their adventure. And best of all for a natural pilot like Conrad, there'd be some true precision flying to do. Armstrong's job had been just to get his lander down safely in the huge Tranquility plain, and he'd succeeded at that, even if he'd overshot the prime landing area by four miles.

Conrad would get no such margin of error. Resting in the Ocean of Storms was a little robot lander named *Surveyor 3*, which NASA had sent to the moon two and a half years earlier.

Conrad was expected to touch down close enough to the old spacecraft that he and Bean could walk to it and remove its camera to take home and study what long-range exposure to the lunar environment did to electronic hardware.

That was the kind of targeted flying worthy of a navy man who had once piloted jet aircraft off of and back onto the heaving decks of aircraft carriers.

First, though, came getting off the ground in Florida, which would require punching through the mess of bad weather that was hanging over the launch site.

At 11:22 a.m., the countdown clock at last wound down to zero, and the five massive engines at the bottom of the rocket stack ignited, producing a combined 7.5 million pounds of thrust.

"Liftoff! The clock is running," Conrad called as the *Saturn V* muscled itself off the pad and the mission clock on the instrument panel began to move.

Conrad, Gordon and Bean had been as prepared as they could be for the shaking and noise of a *Saturn V* launch—but the simulators in which they trained could never match the violence of the real thing. Still, for Conrad, who had flown twice before aboard the far smaller *Gemini Titan* rocket, the *Saturn V*'s powerful ride was a thrill.

"This baby is really going!" he called over the roar.

"Man, is it ever!" Gordon agreed.

"That's a lovely liftoff! Not bad at all!" Conrad enthused.

It stayed lovely, too—but only for another fifteen seconds or so.

Then, just thirty-seven seconds after launch and a mile

and a half into the sky, a flash of light and a loud bang exploded through the cockpit.

"What the hell was that?" Gordon exclaimed.

Instinctively, all three astronauts looked toward the instrument panel, and what they saw shocked them. From one side of the big board to the other, the vital signs of their spacecraft were falling apart. Fuel cells flashed red, electrical systems spiked and failed; guidance programs, onboard computers, life-support systems—basically anything dependent on electricity, which meant everything—began to malfunction. Worst of all, the four gyroscopes, together known as the guidance platform, went completely offline, meaning that the guided missile that was the *Saturn V* was in danger of becoming completely unguided.

"Okay, we just lost the platform, gang," Conrad radioed to the ground. "I don't know what happened here; we had everything in the world drop out."

Then he began to read off what he meant by *everything*.

"I got three fuel cell lights, an AC bus light, a fuel cell disconnect, AC bus overload one and two, Main Bus A and B out."

To TV viewers watching the unfolding disaster at home, it might have been gibberish—but it was clearly very bad.

Worse, to the engineers manning the consoles in Mission Control, it didn't make much sense, either. They had simulated every conceivable emergency during the months of training that led up to the mission, but they had never tried anything like this.

Conrad's left hand was resting on the spacecraft abort

handle. In the event of a launch disaster, it was the commander's call to end the mission and save his crew, activating the escape rockets, which would pull the *Apollo* capsule up and away from the *Saturn V* and send the crew to a safe parachute descent in the Atlantic.

That, of course, would mean the end of a half-billion-dollar rocket and the end, too, of what was supposed to be a ten-day lunar mission, after less than ten minutes.

For the moment, the commander kept his hand still.

Conrad's counterpart in Mission Control was Gerry Griffin, a former guidance and navigation officer who had recently been promoted to flight director—the overall boss of the control room. Now, in his first turn in the lead chair, a moon mission was falling apart around him.

Griffin toggled his microphone open and spoke directly to John Aaron, the twenty-four-year-old engineer sitting at what was known as the EECOM (electrical, environmental and consumables) console.

"How's it looking, EECOM?" he asked. He got no answer. "EECOM, what do you see?" he repeated.

What Aaron was seeing was not good—the same ratty data all of the other controllers had on their screens. Like the other controllers, he had never seen anything like it before— or almost never. Aaron had already developed a reputation as something of a wonder in Mission Control, someone who could make sense of even the most senseless data, and had an uncanny way of remembering nearly any glitch that had ever affected any rocket that had been placed in his care before.

He now recalled a moment a couple of years earlier, when he was manning a console during a simulated launch of a smaller, unmanned *Saturn 1B* rocket. That day he'd seen similarly screwy numbers on his screen—too screwy to be believable— and he guessed the problem could be traced to what was known as the signal conditioning equipment, or SCE.

The job of the SCE was to translate the signals coming from the electrical system into usable data that the controllers and astronauts could read. If the system failed, switching it from its primary mode to its auxiliary mode would reboot the SCE itself and also bring the entire electrical system back online if it had gone off.

The SCE was so rarely used, however, that almost nobody knew what it was. Even in the spacecraft, the switch was installed in an entirely obscure spot, off to the far right of the instrument panel, over Al Bean's right shoulder.

"Flight, EECOM, try SCE to aux," Aaron said to Griffin.

"Say again, SCE to off?" Griffin asked.

"Aux," Aaron repeated. "Auxiliary, Flight."

Griffin then radioed the command to the capcom, who radioed it up to the ship.

"*Apollo 12*, Houston. Try SCE to auxiliary. Over," he said.

Conrad scowled. "FCE to auxiliary? What the hell is that?"

"SCE," the capcom corrected.

Conrad and Gordon did not know where to begin looking for the switch, but Bean, the one rookie aboard, did. He reached up behind himself and threw it to the new setting. Straightaway, the sickly lights and numbers on the instrument panel and the screens in Mission Control began to get well.

"It looks . . . Everything looks good," Bean said tentatively.

Aaron sighed in relief; Griffin, who had been standing, dropped back in his seat.

"Okay, we'll straighten out our problems here," Conrad said as the rocket sped on toward space. "I don't know what happened; I'm not sure we didn't get hit by lightning."

That was exactly what had happened—or almost exactly. It was true that there were no lightning storms directly over the Cape, but as *Apollo 12* passed through the already charged clouds, it turned itself into a one-mile-long lightning rod, attracting a flash that passed through the rocket and ran all the way down the rocket's exhaust trail to the ground. The entire long bolt would be visible later when photos from the automatic launchpad camera were developed.

Still, the *Saturn V* did its work, with its upper stage—the section carrying the *Apollo* spacecraft and the lunar module—finally limping into Earth orbit. Whether the crew would be able to go any farther was still very much in doubt.

Apollo missions on their way to the moon typically made two circuits around the Earth in what was called a parking orbit, while the astronauts checked out their systems before relighting their engine and blasting out toward the moon. Dawdling in orbit any longer would throw off the translunar trajectory and compromise the mission.

That gave *Apollo 12* less than three hours to sort out its multiple messes, the most serious of which concerned the gyroscopes. Even as the spacecraft's electrical systems were slowly straightening themselves out, the guidance platform remained completely offline—and the clock was ticking.

In the back of Mission Control, Chris Kraft, a former flight director and now NASA's overall director of flight operations, watched the scene play out in the normally orderly control center and looked especially closely at Aaron. He walked up to the young EECOM's console and put his hand on his shoulder.

"Son, we don't have to go to the moon today," he said.

Aaron took his meaning. Kraft was saying be careful. He was saying listen to what the systems are telling you. He was saying don't try to be a hero and wind up killing these men. We can always just bring them home.

As it worked out, Aaron was able to bring *Apollo 12* fully back to life, and Gordon, in the spacecraft, was able to realign the gyroscopes—though that part of the job wasn't easy. He had to wait until the orbiting spacecraft had crossed over to the night side of the Earth and then use the timeless mariner's method of taking sightings on stars. That gave him what was known as a rough alignment. Finessing that approximate reading with the aid of the onboard computer gave him what was known as a fine alignment.

When he was done, *Apollo 12* once again knew where it was.

Not long after, the mission was at last given the thumbs-up for the critical engine burn that would carry the astronauts to the moon—the maneuver known as the translunar injection.

"*Apollo 12*, Houston," the capcom said. "The good word is you're go for TLI."

"Hoop-de-doo, we're ready!" Conrad exclaimed. "We didn't expect anything else!"

Four and a half days later, Pete Conrad and Al Bean set their lunar module down in the Ocean of Storms, while Dick Gordon station-kept in the command module orbiting overhead. The two moonwalkers landed their ship just 600 feet from the old *Surveyor* spacecraft.

Conrad, whom history would forever record as merely the second commander to do the thing Neil Armstrong had done before, no longer seemed to mind that status. Indeed, as the shortest man in the astronaut corps—measuring just five foot six—he had decided what his first words would be when he jumped down from the final rung of the lunar module ladder to step on the moon.

"Man," he said, "that may have been a small one for Neil, but that's a long one for me."

The Apollo 13 *service module, seen after it was jettisoned by the crew. An entire panel on the module had been blown off by an explosion four days earlier.*

> EIGHT >

EXPLOSION IN SPACE

Apollo 13, 1970

IT WAS NEVER easy to get Jim Lovell angry, but that didn't mean it was impossible. And right about then, the commander of *Apollo 13* could have pitched Fred Haise straight out into space. Lovell was a veteran of three other space flights and had never before felt like tossing a crewmate overboard. And he was unlikely to stay mad for long. But at the moment, Haise had gotten under his skin.

It had been an exceedingly pleasant two days— actually two days, seven hours and forty-five minutes, according to the mission clock. That was how long it had been since the *Apollo 13* crew had lifted off from the Kennedy Space Center in Florida. Now they were 200,000 miles from Earth, just 40,000 miles from the moon and just a day and a half away from landing on its surface in the Fra Mauro formation, south of the lunar equator.

Lovell was flying with two rookies this trip—Haise in the

right-hand seat and Jack Swigert in the center. It was Haise who would be traveling down to the surface with Lovell in the LEM, which the crew had nicknamed *Aquarius*. Swigert would be remaining in lunar orbit, station-keeping in the command module *Odyssey*.

More so than most astronauts, Lovell was never so happy as when he was in space, and never so happy in space as when he was in command of a mission. It wasn't just that he liked the feel of being in charge of a spacecraft. He also liked the feel of being equal parts mentor and trail guide for his junior crewmates. At forty-two, he was only four years older than Swigert and six years older than Haise, but from the moment of liftoff he found himself looking after the first-timers, helping them to manage the challenges of traveling in space, as well as appreciate the singular joys.

"Jack, be careful in your movements now," he warned shortly after the spacecraft reached Earth orbit and Swigert unbuckled from his seat and began drifting around the cabin. Newcomers to the roomy *Apollo* spacecraft often got space-sick when they first began to move about in zero-g; Lovell himself had had to take some steadying breaths and keep his eyes ahead when he flew to the moon on Apollo 8's lunar orbital mission seventeen months earlier.

Even before the current crew got to space, there were lessons for the commander to teach. Lovell was prepared for the violent way he'd be thrown forward in his seat restraints a few minutes after liftoff, when the *Saturn V*'s first stage cut off and the second stage lit. The rest of his crew hadn't been.

"When that shut down, man, I thought I was going through the instrument panel," Haise said after that phase of the mission had passed.

"I should have warned you," Lovell answered, and he meant it. The ten days the crew would be in space would be tough enough without the other two men being surprised by anything.

Now, however, in the first several hours of the mission's third day, it was Haise who had surprised him. It was about 9:00 p.m. East Coast time on April 13, which meant 8:00 p.m. spacecraft time, since the ship set its clocks to match the ones in Houston. Whatever the precise hour, it was prime time for the TV networks across much of the country, and NASA had scheduled a live broadcast from translunar space for people following the mission back home.

Of course, it was not a sure thing that many TV viewers were following the mission back home. During the *Apollo 8* crew's six days in space, the audience for their broadcasts had been global. It was the first time human beings had orbited the moon, and on Christmas Eve 1968, when Lovell, Frank Borman and Bill Anders beamed a show home from just sixty nautical miles above the lunar surface, the networks estimated that close to a billion people watched—or just shy of one-third of the entire human species.

Things were similar seven months later, when *Apollo 11* achieved the first lunar landing. But *Apollo 12* had flown since then, *Apollo 13* was flying now and *Apollos 14* through *19* were coming up later. The human attention span can be a fleeting thing, and TV shows of people flying to the moon did not quite have the power to engage that they once did. Still, Lovell, Swigert and Haise would put on the best performance they could, and when the camera went on, Lovell in particular worked hard to play host.

"What we plan to do for today," he said, "is to start out in the spaceship *Odyssey*, and take you on through from *Odyssey* in through the tunnel to *Aquarius*."

He delivered on that promise, and for the next thirty-one minutes toured the two spacecraft in detail, showing off the sleeping area, the navigation station, the view through the windows and especially the interior of the lunar module, which would be his and Haise's home and lifeline when they were descending to and returning from the moon.

After half an hour of the indoor travelogue, Lovell drifted from the lunar module back to the command module and prepared to sign off, leaving Haise behind to power down the LEM for the night. Part of that job involved pushing a black plunger in the lunar module that would equalize the pressure between the two vehicles.

There were two ways to push the plunger: soft and hard. Both ways did precisely the same job, but soft did it silently, while hard produced a loud but harmless bang.

Haise loved the bang—and he loved, too, the way it startled anyone not prepared for it. From the lunar module, he heard Lovell wrapping up.

"Any time you want to terminate, we're all set to go," Lovell said to the controllers in Houston and, by extension, to the people watching at home. Then he added, "We've just got to put the cabin repress valve in."

Haise, hearing that, smiled a mischievous smile and then put the cabin repress valve in but good. The predicted bang shook the ships, and the startled response from Lovell and Swigert followed.

Lovell glowered down the tunnel toward Haise. "Every time he does that, our hearts jump in our mouths," he said, unamused.

In Houston, the capcom astronaut Jack Lousma heard the change in tone and sought to keep things light.

"Okay, Jim. It's been a really good show. We think we ought to conclude it from here."

"Sounds good," Lovell said. "This is the crew of *Apollo 13* wishing everybody there a nice evening. We're just about ready to close out our inspection of *Aquarius* and get back for a pleasant evening in *Odyssey*."

With that, the program ended.

As history would note, it would not in fact be a pleasant evening in *Odyssey*. History would note specifically that just over nine minutes later, there would be another bang aboard *Apollo 13*, louder, more violent than the earlier one—one that was not the result of a junior crewman playing a prank, but an explosion in an onboard oxygen tank that would blow the side of *Odyssey* off, cripple the ship and leave the crew effectively marooned in deep space.

The unlikely survival of the *Apollo 13* crew and the inge-nuity and imagination it took to get them home is a celebrated tale. More than 200,000 miles from Earth, the explosion in one of *Odyssey*'s oxygen tanks would cause a crack in the second one, leaving the spacecraft completely without the key element it needed not only to allow the astronauts to breathe but to power the ship's fuel cells, which provided it with electricity. The spacecraft was effectively dead, which could easily have left the astronauts dead as well.

But *Odyssey* wasn't the only spacecraft the crew had. They also had the lunar excursion module, nicknamed *Aquarius*. The LEM was a very fragile ship, with walls no thicker than three sheets of aluminum foil. It could get two of the three astronauts down to the lunar surface and back up to the *Odyssey* waiting in orbit, but it was nowhere near sturdy enough to get all three of them home and to reenter through the Earth's atmosphere. Still, *Aquarius* had its own engines and its own oxygen and electricity, and the crew could use it as a sort of onboard lifeboat over the next four days, as they whipped around the moon and came home, fighting the whole way to get enough life back into *Odyssey* to allow them to splash down safely in the ocean.

The astronauts are often thought of as the heroes of this mission, and they were, but they were not the only ones. Just as important were the dozens of people in Mission Control who fought to figure out the spacecraft's problems on the fly, in real time, while the mortal clock ticked for the men in space.

Their story is less well-known, but it played out dramatically—in face-to-face conversations and on private communications loops—as they sought to manage an emergency none of them had even imagined could occur. Everything that unfolded in space would turn on the decisions made in the first few hours. And those decisions, in the fullness of time, would turn out to have been the right ones.

The bang that shook *Apollo 13* and ended what should have been the third lunar landing occurred precisely fifty-five hours, fifty-four minutes and fifty-three seconds into the mission and was initiated by the most routine of procedures, requested by a Mission Controller named Sy Liebergot. Liebergot manned the EECOM console. That acronym (for electrical, environmental and consumables manager, the same position that played so important a role after the *Apollo 12* lightning strike) was just one more in a Mission Control that was full of them: there was FIDO, for flight dynamics officer; GUIDO, for guidance officer; GNC, for guidance navigation and control and on and on. But the EECOM had a special responsibility.

It was the systems he oversaw—the oxygen, the power, the water flow, the heaters, the coolant loops—that ensured that the spacecraft remained a habitable, survivable place. The FIDO and the GUIDO could send you to space and bring you home, but it was the EECOM who would have to keep you alive for the journey.

On the evening of April 13, Liebergot was wrapping up his workday and looking forward to handing off the EECOM console to the next shift. It was something of a matter of professional pride for every team to pass on a spacecraft in the best condition possible, and one of the routine items on Liebergot's to-do list tonight was to request what was known as a cryo stir.

There were two tanks of liquid oxygen and two tanks of liquid hydrogen aboard the ship. The oxygen provided the astronauts with air to breathe, and both the oxygen and the hydrogen fed the onboard fuel cells, which generated the ship's electricity. Supercold liquids that sit too long, however, tend to stratify, with a slushy layer separating from a liquid layer.

To keep things uniform, and thus ensure a smooth flow of oxygen and hydrogen into the spacecraft systems, each tank was equipped with a fan that would be switched on every few hours for a quick mixing.

Now, as the night shift prepared to come on duty, Liebergot called Gene Kranz, the flight director on duty, and asked him in turn to call Lousma and request the stir.

"Capcom," Kranz said in response. "Looks like the last item we need here is a stir on the H_2 and O_2 at their convenience."

"Thirteen, we've got one more item for you when you get a chance," Lousma relayed. "We'd like you to stir up your cryo tanks."

That command was meant for Swigert. As command module pilot, he would not be landing on the moon's surface with Lovell and Haise two days hence, but he would make it his business to ensure that they had a fit ship to come back to.

"Okay," Swigert answered. "Stand by."

As Lovell and Haise went about other business, Swigert reached for the instrument panel and threw the four switches that would turn on the fans in the tanks. In three of those tanks, the fans responded as they were designed to, spinning into motion silently and swiftly. In one of those tanks, oxygen tank two, the fan started to do the same—but it would finish very differently.

Unknown to anyone on the ground or aboard the ship, deep inside the tank was a single bad wire connected to the fan. Its Teflon insulation had been burned away weeks earlier when a blown circuit breaker had caused the tank to overheat during a routine test on the pad. The problem had gone undetected, and the spacecraft was certified fit to fly—despite the fact that it was manifestly unfit.

When Swigert flipped the tank two switch, a spark flew, and a spark in a tank of liquid oxygen is even worse than a spark in a tank of gasoline. Immediately, the oxygen ignited and the tank exploded. The blast, in turn, blew an entire panel off of the exterior of the spacecraft, and in that violence, oxygen tank one was damaged, too—a small but critical crack forming in its surface.

Inside the cockpit, it was impossible to know what had just happened, but it was impossible to miss the fact that it was something terrible. A bang and a shudder tore through both *Odyssey* and the attached *Aquarius*. At the same time a caution and warning alarm sounded.

Haise was in the tunnel that connected the ships at the moment of the blast and actually saw the walls around him torque and twist. Lovell immediately looked down the tunnel and flashed him a glare, assuming it was the cursed repress valve again. But when he caught the rookie's eyes, he saw not playfulness there, but alarm.

"It wasn't me," Haise said hoarsely.

Lovell turned to the instrument panel and saw nothing short of catastrophe playing out. Every light, it seemed, was flashing red; every gauge was jumping high or falling low; the spacecraft itself was gyrating wildly, and the instrument panel compass was swinging in response. Swigert had already scanned the panel and keyed open his mic.

"Okay, Houston, we've had a problem," he called.

"This is Houston, say again, please," Lousma answered.

"Houston, we've had a problem," Lovell repeated.

"Okay, stand by, Thirteen, we're looking at it," Lousma said.

Liebergot, specifically, was the one doing the looking, and he was as alarmed and mystified as the astronauts were. According to his readings, one of the spacecraft's two main electrical distribution systems, known as Bus B, had crashed, shutting down half of the spacecraft's power, which in turn led to the flood of other system failures.

Oxygen tank two, meantime, seemed somehow not to exist, with its pressure, temperature and voltage levels all reading zero. Oxygen tank one was still there, but its pressure, which should have been over 600 pounds per square inch, was slowly falling. What's more, of the spacecraft's three fuel cells, only number two appeared to be working. Cells one and three were flickering—and on the way to failing entirely.

To Liebergot, so huge a storm of seemingly unrelated breakdowns was actually a cause for comfort. Two or three anomalies that were causally connected could certainly happen, but everything breaking down at once suggested a problem known as instrumentation. In those cases, the spacecraft itself was fine; it was the sensors that monitored it that had failed, sending home all manner of bogus readings that made no collective sense. Resetting the sensors was usually all it took to set things right.

Before Liebergot could call Kranz and share his thinking, he heard a call in his headset.

"What's the matter with the data, EECOM?" the voice asked.

The question came from Larry Sheaks, part of the EECOM's backroom team, the group of technicians who would trouble-shoot problems and pass recommendations on to the man on the main room. Liebergot suspected Sheaks was thinking the same thing he was thinking.

"Larry, you don't believe that O_2 tank pressure, do you?" he asked.

"No, no," Sheaks responded as he scanned the rest of the instrument panel. "Manifold's good; environmental control system is good."

That reassured Liebergot. "Okay, Flight," he said to Kranz. "We've got some instrumentation. Let me add 'em up."

"Rog," was all Kranz answered, a term he often used when he was too busy even for a full "Roger."

Up in the spacecraft, Lovell, Swigert and Haise were also clinging to the thin hope that the problem was instrumentation. By now Haise had pushed out of the tunnel and begun scanning the instrument panel, and noticed that Main Bus B appeared to be rallying, coming back online and producing at least a tentative stream of power.

"Okay, right now, Houston, the voltage is looking good," he said with a trace of relief. What was more, for a moment at least, the instruments indicated that oxygen tank two was functioning again. That was impossible since the tank no longer existed, but somehow it had left a ghost of itself in the data stream.

"It was oscillating down about twenty to sixty percent, but now it's full-scale high again," Haise reported.

Then, however, Haise added one more detail—a detail that couldn't be dismissed as instrumentation, unless the instruments to blame were the very hearing and physical senses of the astronauts themselves. "We had a pretty large bang associated with the caution and warning there," he said.

"Roger, Fred," Lousma answered flatly.

Even the bang, however, did not entirely rule out instrumentation. Perhaps the spacecraft had taken a glancing hit by a passing meteor that did it little harm but jolted its sensors. That might also account for the ship's oscillations. Kranz, it seemed, was ready to consider such a way around the apparent mess.

"Let's get some recommendations here, Sy," he said. "Have you got a sick sensor there or what?"

Liebergot did not know, and answered instead with a recommendation for Lovell. According to the EECOM's readings, Bus A, the other half of *Apollo 13*'s power distribution system, was faltering, too, but was at least functioning, thanks to fuel cell two, which was still in the game. Perhaps switching the two sickly fuel cells to the opposite buses would reconfigure the entire power system enough to jolt it all awake.

It would be an inelegant fix—a little like having an electrical problem at home and trying out different plugs in different wall outlets until you found a combination that worked. You might not know exactly what was causing all the trouble, but at least you'd have power.

"Fuel cells one and three are offline," Liebergot said to Kranz. "Have him attempt to reconnect one to Main A and three to Main B."

"Okay, fuel cell one . . . ," Kranz repeated, writing the recommendation down before transmitting it to Lousma.

". . . back to Main A, fuel cell three back to Main B," Liebergot finished for him.

Kranz passed the instruction to Lousma, who passed it on to the spacecraft, and Swigert threw the appropriate switches. A moment later he called back down—and his report was bleak.

"Okay, Houston," he radioed, "I tried to reset, and fuel [cells] one and three are both showing zip on the flows."

Liebergot frowned and then did the only thing he could do, which was to turn the last suggestion around: connecting fuel cells one and three to the buses the opposite way.

"Flight, EECOM," he said.

"Go, EECOM," Kranz answered.

"Let's reverse the configuration request," Liebergot began, but Kranz cut him off.

"Wait a minute," he snapped, "we've got a good Main A Bus; let's make sure that whatever we do doesn't screw up Main A."

Liebergot assured him that that wouldn't happen, and the command was radioed up to the ship. Swigert executed the command and called down to report that the situation, again, remained unchanged. Lovell then called down to the capcom with more bad news.

"And, Jack, our O_2 quantity number two tank is reading zero," he said. "Did you get that?"

Lousma confirmed that he did. Whatever spectral readings tank two had left behind when it died were now gone.

Kranz, who never minded showing his exasperation when a ship was behaving badly, showed it now.

"Can we review our status here, Sy, and see what we've got from a standpoint of status?" he asked. And then, in case that wasn't specific enough, he got to the nut of the matter. "What do you think we've got in the spacecraft that's good?"

By now, Liebergot knew the answer was "not much." In addition to all of the other problems *Odyssey* was facing, the explosion had shut the valves on some of its thrusters, meaning that no matter how deftly Lovell maneuvered the spacecraft, it kept gyrating, and he could not bring it to heel.

Communications were flickering in and out as well, partly due to the uncontrolled tumbling, partly due to the fact that when its side panel was blasted away, the debris collided with the high-gain antenna, breaking its radio lock with the Earth.

The power, meantime, was still failing and, most troubling of all, the oxygen supply in tank one—which was all the oxygen *Odyssey* had left—was approaching a critical state. Its pressure was down to just 318 pounds per square inch, meaning that more than half of what had been available an hour ago had now leaked into space.

In the ship, Lovell read the gauge and nudged Swigert, who hailed Lousma at the capcom station. "Jack," he said, "are you copying O_2 tank one cryo pressure?"

"That's affirmative," Lousma answered.

The rest of the controllers, Kranz included, were copying it, too.

Kranz called to the backroom team that oversaw Mission Control's Real-Time Computing Complex, or RTCC, which was the basement facility where the mainframe computers were kept.

"Bring me up another computer in the RTCC, will you?" he said. "And I want a bunch of guys capable of running de-logs down there." He was asking not only for computer brainpower but for the human brainpower needed to read the recorded data streams, the de-logs, that had been coming from the spacecraft since before launch and scour them for clues to what had gone wrong.

Whether there would be time for such forensic work before the spacecraft died, however, was unclear— something Liebergot understood better than anyone else. It was time, he knew, to ask the question that had been playing around the edge of his mind for the past ten minutes—and, he suspected, was on a lot of other minds both on the ground and in the spacecraft, too.

"Flight, EECOM," he said, "the pressure on O_2 tank one is all the way down to two ninety-seven; we'd better think about getting in the LEM."

There was, at first, no response, and that made sense.

Liebergot was calling for the desperation exercise known as the lifeboat scenario, the business of giving up on a disabled ship, sheltering in place in a working one and buying time to figure out where to go from there. Kranz, like many other people at NASA, had considered the lifeboat exercise casually but had never believed he'd have to use it, and he still wasn't quite ready to try. "Got any more suggestions?" he bluntly asked.

"No," Liebergot answered, his voice for the first time betraying a trace of despair. "We're gonna hit one hundred PSI in an hour and fifty-four minutes. That's the end right there."

Kranz thought silently for a full two minutes. He knew that even if the LEM could sustain the *Apollo 13* astronauts for the next three or four days, he'd still have to come up with a way to bring the command module back to life at the end of the mission, since that was the only part of the paired spacecraft that could safely reenter the Earth's atmosphere.

He knew, too, that before *Apollo 13* could get closer to home, it would have to get farther away—whipping first around the far side of the moon. And he knew that any engine burns the trip home required would have to be handled by the LEM, since *Odyssey*'s engine could not be trusted to light or, if it did light, to do so without blowing up.

But those poor options were the only ones he had. Even before announcing anything to the room, he made up his mind. He then opened his mic and called Bill Stoval, the flight dynamics officer.

"Whatever planning you do," he said, "I want to do assuming we're going around the moon and we're using the LEM for performing the maneuver, because in the present configuration, unless we get a heck of a lot smarter, I think we're wasting our time planning on using the SPS."

"And I'm assuming you want fastest possible return," Stoval said.

"Yeah, I think that's the case," Kranz answered.

It would still be another half hour before Mission Control and the *Apollo 13* crew would learn what the flight director had decided. At last, however, Lousma radioed up the news both to the astronauts and to the outside world, which was now very much following the flight of *Apollo 13*.

"We're starting to think about the LEM lifeboat," Lousma informed Lovell, Swigert and Haise.

"Yes," said Swigert, the command module pilot, who would soon have no command module at all, "that's what we're thinking about, too."

Before two more hours had elapsed, the LEM was powered up, the command module was put into a deep, cold sleep and the three-man crew huddled together in the two-person lander.

In the end, that fastest route possible that Kranz had hoped for would take three and a half more days, over the course of which procedures would be invented in the moment, maneuvers would be executed that had never even been simulated and the astronauts would jury-rig repairs from little more than plastic wrap and duct tape and whatever other supplies they had on hand.

Kranz would take a few moments over those days to meet with the clamoring press corps, and each time he did he would be asked if he really believed he could save the crew. Whenever he got that question, he answered the same way: *These men are coming home*, he'd say. *We don't know exactly when, we don't know exactly how and we don't know how much spacecraft we'll have left, but we'll get them back.*

In the years that followed, Kranz would wonder if that sounded like bravado, or worse, like arrogance. But three and a half days later, on April 17, at 2:07 p.m. Houston time, he made good on his pledge, as *Apollo 13*, with three happy crewmen riding one tough command module, splashed down safely in the Pacific. It ain't bragging if you can do it, went the old baseball quote. And Kranz, along with the three astronauts and the thousands of other people in the space community who sent them aloft, did it indeed.

A Soyuz *reentry has its moments of serenity. On the long-ago flight of* Soyuz 11, *the silent spacecraft held a terrible secret.*

> NINE >

THE THREE LOST COSMONAUTS

Soyuz 11, 1971

ALEXEI LEONOV DID not like the look he saw in Viktor Patsayev's eyes. That was not entirely a surprise. Patsayev was thirty-seven years old, but he had an older man's eyes—gray-green, always sad, set under eyebrows that were arched in a look of slight worry.

Tonight, though, should have been a very good night for Patsayev. It was June 3, 1971, and the two men, along with the other four members of *Soyuz 11*'s prime crew and backup crew, were in the cosmonaut quarters at the Baikonur Cosmodrome in Kazakhstan. In only three days, Patsayev had just learned, he'd be going to space.

The Western press in Europe and the United States never tired of describing Baikonur as the sort of belly of the Soviet beast—a dark and secretive place where the Communist Russian empire worked to project its power into the high ground of space. That was true enough as far as it went, but it didn't go very far. To look at Baikonur was to see not a great center of global intrigue, but something closer to a college campus—with groves and lanes of poplar trees, two-story office buildings that could have just as easily held classrooms and clapboard dwellings that could just as easily have been dorms.

Somewhere in the distance was the iron ring of security gates and, behind them, the fearsome stand of launchpads that sent the rockets into space, but in the middle of it all was a sense of ease and peace. At the moment, however, there was nothing easy or peaceful about the mood in the cosmonaut quarters.

Until this very morning, Leonov—who had already made history as the first human being to walk in space, three months before Ed White on the *Gemini 4*—had been set to command the next great rocket that would leave Baikonur, taking off aboard *Soyuz 11* for a one-month stay aboard the new *Salyut 1* space station. That would be a very big achievement for the Soviet Union.

The US might have won the race to the moon, and indeed, the very next month, *Apollo 15* was set to make yet another lunar landing for the Americans. But that was all theater—the pretty business of flags and footprints and a few dozen pounds of rocks. The true scientific, engineering and military work would be done in low Earth orbit, where the first country to establish a permanent lab and habitat would be the true space power.

Salyut 1 would be an important step toward staking that claim. The station was a magnificent thing, a sixty-foot-long spaceliner with three different habitable compartments and so much room that it actually had a treadmill aboard to keep the cosmonauts fit. Leonov and his two-man crew, Valeri Kubasov and Pyotr Kolodin, were thrilled to have been given the opportunity to fly it in the service of the Soviet nation.

But just that day, when the doctors were conducting their final preflight exams of the crew, they found something troubling in one of Kubasov's X-rays. It was a shadow in his right lung, as big as an egg and impossible to miss. It didn't look like a tumor—which was very good news for Kubasov—but it did look like tuberculosis, which was very bad news for not just him but for Leonov and Kolodin, too.

Tumors, after all, aren't contagious, but tuberculosis is. And while all six members of the prime and backup crew had spent time in one another's company over the past few weeks, it was Leonov and Kolodin who had spent the most time with the sick man.

The doctors made the only call they thought they could: the entire prime crew would be grounded, and the entire backup crew would take their place.

Leonov fumed and told the doctors what he thought of their plan, but they were unmovable, and the commander had no choice but to relent. As night fell, he and the other five cosmonauts retreated to the crew quarters so the original prime crew could brief their replacements. Leonov would take the lead, reviewing the *Salyut* systems with the new commander, Georgi Dobrovolsky, as well as with Patsayev and the third crew member, Vladislav Volkov.

Detail by detail, he walked the other cosmonauts through the danger points in the mission, from launch through docking with the space station, through the thirty days aloft and, finally, through reentry. And then, almost as an afterthought, he remembered one more thing that troubled him about the *Soyuz* spacecraft: the vents that kept the cabin pressurized during the plunge from space. They were supposed to be closed and sealed automatically before reentry, but Leonov never fully trusted any spacecraft to do anything automatically when a cosmonaut could do it himself.

"Close the air vents by hand," he told the new crew, "then open them by hand when you're on the ground."

The other three cosmonauts nodded and made a note of the instruction, and Leonov, at last satisfied, signaled the end of the meeting and allowed them all to go to bed. Something about the evening was nagging at him, however. It was, he realized, Patsayev—particularly a haunted look he'd seen cross the younger cosmonaut's face.

When Leonov was troubled by something, he liked to lose himself in his artwork, and was a good enough painter that he could have made a career as an artist if space hadn't claimed him first. In the quiet of the crew quarters, he took a piece of notepaper and a pencil from his desk and sketched the face he'd seen that night. He titled it "Patsayev's Eyes." And then he put it away.

Whatever reason Patsayev or anyone else at Baikonur had to worry about the first mission to the *Salyut 1* space station dissipated at least a little just before 8:00 on the morning of June 6, when the twenty engines of the reliable *Soyuz* rocket lit and the big missile did what it had been doing successfully for four years now, which was to get a three-person *Soyuz* spacecraft safely to orbit. The *Soyuz* would link to the *Salyut* in the same way the Americans' *Gemini* spacecraft linked with the *Agena*. And like the *Agena*, the *Salyut* had been launched into space aboard its own rocket and was patiently orbiting there, waiting for cosmonauts to arrive.

Less than ten minutes after they left the pad, the cosmonauts were in space. A day after that, they had chased down the *Salyut*, linked up with it easily and climbed aboard. Straightaway, it was clear to the crew that the world's first space station was every bit the luxury liner the designers had intended it to be.

The three compartments measured thirteen feet across at their widest point—more than ample for a bedroom in an apartment in Moscow, the Soviet Union's capital, which is what the cosmonauts were used to. No fewer than seven different instrument panels lined the walls of the station, providing eight different work stations depending on what job a cosmonaut had to do at any moment. The ship was outfitted with its own observatory, capable of capturing visible and ultraviolet images of stars and other bodies. Patsayev was the mission astronomer, and the moment he peered through the eyepiece at his first target star, he would become the first person in history to operate a telescope above the thick, obscuring blanket of Earth's atmosphere. Patsayev's sad eyes would see some very happy things.

There was something else about the *Salyut*, too: it was beautiful. Four solar panels extended from the sides of the ship like great wings, appearing almost to be keeping the twenty-ton machine flying in the airlessness of space. When the smaller *Soyuz*, with its own pair of wings, was docked to the front, the entire assembly took on an almost delicate, dragonfly look.

The Soviets were justifiably proud of what they had built and made the uncharacteristic decision to show it off. Every day the *Soyuz 11* crew was in space, the astronauts would appear live on TV throughout the Soviet Union, where they instantly became national celebrities. Patsayev turned thirty-eight on the crew's thirteenth day in space, and his birthday was celebrated across the country. Dobrovolsky, the commander who had been called in at the last moment to lead the mission, was informally pronounced a national hero. And Volkov, with his dark, movie-star smolder, became an idol of teenage girls, who clipped his picture from magazines and tacked it to their bedroom walls the way girls in Europe and America did with famous musicians like the Beatles and the Rolling Stones.

But all was not going as well aboard *Salyut 1* as the TV broadcasts would make it seem, and the problems began almost immediately. No sooner had the cosmonauts climbed aboard the station than they noticed an acrid smell caused by a failed air filter. There was no way of knowing exactly what toxins might be fouling the cabin atmosphere, so the cosmonauts spent their first full night at *Salyut* sleeping in the attached *Soyuz*, while the environmental control scrubbers attempted to clear the air.

Throughout at least a portion of their time aloft, the crew was supposed to wear so-called penguin suits—pressure garments that were intended to improve blood flow and counteract the absence of gravity. The suits, however, did not seem to do a thing for their circulation, and the elastic bands that provided the pressure kept breaking. The cosmonauts' lung capacity, the maximum amount of air they could forcefully breathe out, declined by more than 30 percent over the first two weeks, a sign that long-term weightlessness was harder on the body than it seemed.

Making things worse, the key piece of equipment that was intended to counteract some of those ill effects—the treadmill—they dared not use. Bungee cords kept the astronauts tethered to the device, but the thumping of their feet against the tread caused the entire station to shake and the solar wings to flap ominously. It would do the crew no good to improve their lung capacity and blood pressure if the station on which they were depending for their lives was damaged in the process.

Finally, on the sixteenth day in space, when the cosmonauts were busy with astronomical and biomedical experiments, the entire mission nearly came undone. Volkov was working at one of the lab stations when he noticed another sharp smell, this time coming from the rear of the spacecraft. He whipped around and saw a fire in the midst of a nest of equipment. Patsayev and Dobrovolsky saw it at almost the same instant, but it was Volkov who keyed open his microphone first.

"Aboard the station!" he alerted the ground. "It is the curtain!"

That was a nonsense sentence that was supposed to make complete sense to the ground. Consumed by a need for secrecy—the TV broadcasts from the station notwithstanding—the Soviets had drilled both the cosmonauts and Mission Controllers in a series of code words for various onboard emergencies, lest the Americans or some other Western agents be listening in on the air-to-ground channel and spread the negative press.

But what was important to the strategists in Moscow was unimportant to the men who were responsible for flying the mission, and no sooner did the controllers and crew memorize the code words than they promptly began to forget them.

"Please repeat, *Salyut*," came the confused voice from the ground.

"There is a fire on board!" Volkov shouted. That time the ground understood.

The cosmonauts managed to put out the flames quickly, but the near-disaster sent a burst of terror through the Mission Controllers. American controllers had heard the same words coming from the three astronauts in *Apollo 1* during their practice run on the launchpad years before, and all three had died before they could be rescued. The Soviet controllers did not want the same thing to happen on their watch.

The *Salyut* had not been intended to be anything like a permanent facility. It would serve as home to another *Soyuz* crew or two before being replaced by something bigger in the coming years. If both the *Soyuz 11* cosmonauts and the station were wearing down, best to end this mission early, recover the crew safely and determine if the *Salyut* was fit for the planned visit of *Soyuz 12* in another two or three months.

The call was thus made to pull the plug early. The *Soyuz 11* crew would get till their twenty-third day—just one week shy of the planned thirty—and the Soviets would then declare victory and bring them home.

It was about dinnertime in Moscow on that twenty-third day when the cosmonauts drifted into their *Soyuz* and prepared for a reentry that would take them to a precise landing near the town of Jezkazgan in Kazakhstan. Almost immediately, however, it became clear that even this relatively straightforward exercise would not be easy. When the cosmonauts settled into their seats and closed the hatch, a single, troubling light remained illuminated on their instrument panel—the one that told them that while their hatch might be closed, it was not sealed.

That would be a problem not just because it might let the flames of reentry leak inside the spacecraft, but because it would definitely let the atmosphere inside leak out. Ordinarily, space suits would have made such an emergency survivable, but the *Soyuz 11* cosmonauts had no suits. The spacecraft was robust enough that nobody actually expected it to spring a leak on liftoff or reentry, and it was small enough that the only way for three people to fit inside anyway was for them to fly in simple jumpsuits.

Jumpsuits, however, were useless against the vacuum of space, and if the *Soyuz 11* crew could not seal their hatch, they would be in an exceedingly bad spot—unable to stay in orbit indefinitely, but unable to come home, either.

Dobrovolsky tried the hatch again, opening it, slamming it shut and rotating the handle firmly to its closed position. But the light stayed on. He tried again, and the light stayed on again.

The ground, suspecting that the problem might be not with the latch but with the electric sensors that were supposed to indicate when the seal was secure, recommended that Dobrovolsky try wiping a clean cloth all the way around the hatch rim to clear any debris that might be disrupting the signal. He did as instructed—and still the light remained on.

Finally, a controller in Moscow came up with a solution. He had isolated the problem in a single sensor that was not making contact when the door was closed, sending the false signal that the hatch was loose. The crew was instructed to fix the problem with a piece of insulating tape placed over the sensor to close the tiny gap that was preventing the contact. Dobrovolsky complied, closed the hatch and this time the light went off.

The dinner hour in Moscow had by now slipped to nearly 9:30 p.m., but at last the crew was able to cast off and fly free. Three orbits later, when they were soaring in their *Soyuz* high over Chile, Dobrovolsky fired his engine, and his ship began its slow plunge to the ground.

"We are beginning the descent procedure," he called to Moscow.

"Goodbye, *Yantar*," the controller answered, using the spacecraft's call sign, which meant *amber*. "We will see you on mother Earth."

"Prepare cognac," Volkov added with a laugh.

And then the line went dead.

The sudden silence from space was always unsettling, but it was entirely predictable. The heat that is generated by reentry causes all spacecraft to be surrounded by a thick, pink-and-white cloud of superheated plasma, which makes radio communication impossible. The blackout typically lasts three to four minutes, meaning that during what might be the most harrowing part of any mission the crew is entirely on their own. The Soviets and Americans had gotten used to the long, fraught silence, but that didn't make it any less disturbing.

The *Soyuz 11* blackout passed through its first minute and then its second and then its third, as the ship inscribed a descending arc northeast across the Atlantic, over the Southern European coast and toward the Kazakh desert. At the end of the fourth minute, there was still no signal—which was not uncommon, since everything from wind to the precise angle at which a ship reentered meant that the precise time of the blackout could only be estimated.

But the fourth minute became a fifth and the fifth became a sixth, and as still no word came from the spacecraft, tension mounted in the control center. Suddenly, word flashed in from radar stations in Eastern Europe that the spacecraft had been spotted on a straight and true trajectory arcing directly through Kazakhstan toward its Jezkazgan landing site—where the Soviets landed their rockets instead of the ocean, the way Americans do. The men in Mission Control could at last draw breath—but only briefly. The ship might be where it was supposed to be, but if it was, that meant it was well below the point where the plasma should have subsided and a radio channel with the crew should have been reestablished. Still, however, there was only silence from the ship.

The ground hailed the crew repeatedly, but there was no response. The problem could easily be that the radio had simply gone offline during the violent reentry. That was what the controllers told themselves and told themselves during the continued silence, and that was what they believed when the encouraging call came from one of the recovery helicopters converging on the landing site that they had sighted the *Soyuz 11* parachute. Then came an even happier call: "It has landed," the rescuer said. "Our helicopters are nearby."

The Mission Controllers could hear the whupping of the chopper blades over the radio, and they knew that what they were supposed to do now was to say nothing at all while the recovery crew did their job. That job involved approaching the still-hot spacecraft, knocking on the hull to signal the astronauts, rolling the ship if necessary so that they could reach the hatch, then opening it up and helping the cosmonauts out.

What the men in Mission Control were waiting for was a single call from the helicopter crews that would consist of three numbers ranging from five to one, indicating each cosmonaut's condition. A five would mean that the cosmonaut was fit and well. A four would mean slight injuries, and a three or a two would mean more serious injuries. A one would mean a crew member had died.

No word at all came from the field at first, and then, finally, the line crackled open.

"One, one, one," said the voice at the other end. The entire *Soyuz 11* crew was dead.

Utter silence—far grimmer than the one that had been coming back from space—filled Mission Control, and that was awful enough. For the recovery crew themselves, the actual discovery of the state of the crew had been even worse. When they reached the ship, they knocked on its hull and were immediately alarmed when they did not hear any knock in response. They quickly turned the *Soyuz* on its side, opened the hatch and found all three men strapped in their couches, exactly where they should be, but gray and entirely unresponsive.

They clambered to extract the cosmonauts and found Patsayev and Volkov cold to the touch; Dobrovolsky was warmer, so he was pulled out first and laid on the ground and cardiopulmonary resuscitation was performed—but it was far too late for that. Patsayev and Volkov were brought out and laid next to their commander. Then they were lifted into the helicopters and flown to Jezkazgan airport, where a small welcoming celebration of figs and sweet fried dough served by girls in colorful traditional dress had been prepared for them. There would be no celebration today.

Autopsies of the crew would be conducted, but they didn't need to be. The men had died of asphyxiation, or a lack of oxygen, caused by sudden depressurization of the *Soyuz*.

An investigation of the accident, however, showed that the balky hatch had not been responsible. Before the *Soyuz* reentry pod descended into the atmosphere, it had to jettison now-useless modules at its front and back end. The separation was achieved with the aid of explosive bolts—small bits of controlled ordnance that do a very good job of blowing away unneeded parts of spacecraft but pack a concussive punch in the process. When the bolts fired, they jolted open an air vent in the ship—the very vent Leonov had urged the crew to close by hand before reentry.

The crew, however, had not remembered that instruction. Perhaps if they had, they would have noticed that the vent was not fully secured; perhaps not. As it was, the forensic scientists determined that the open vent did its deadly work quickly; just 115 seconds after the modules were jettisoned, a complete vacuum filled the ship, killing the cosmonauts almost immediately. They had been dead for thirty minutes before they ever reached the ground.

Georgi Dobrovolsky, Vladislav Volkov and Viktor Patsayev were given state funerals, and their ashes were interred in the wall of the Kremlin, the main building that housed the Soviet government, along with other heroes of the Soviet Union. The vents on the *Soyuz* spacecraft were redesigned to be leakproof, and the interior of the cockpit was expanded to carry three fully space-suited cosmonauts. Until that work could be completed, the *Soyuz* would be limited to carrying just two suited people. The Americans took heed of the Soviets' tragedy, too, and the next month, when the *Apollo 15* crew flew to the moon, astronauts Dave Scott and Jim Irwin were ordered to wear their pressure suits during both descent to and ascent from the lunar surface.

While they were on the moon, Scott and Irwin took a moment to remember the high price that could be paid in their unlikely business. They had brought with them a small figurine of a fallen astronaut and a plaque with the names of the fourteen Americans and Soviets who had died in the cause of the exploration of space. They laid both of them gently in the lunar soil. The *Soyuz 11* crew, who never quite achieved their full month in space, would have an eternal presence there all the same.

A two-fingered fireball formed when the Challenger *spacecraft and its main fuel tank exploded and its solid-fuel rockets flew on. The image is one of the most searing in the history of space flight.*

> TEN >

THE LOST TEACHER

Challenger, 1986

WHEN YOU'RE IN Concord, New Hampshire, in the thick of January, you've got a right to be in a lousy mood. If the cold doesn't get to you, the gray skies will; if it's not the gray, it's the short days and the damp air and the snow that doesn't seem to quit. The holidays may have gotten you through December, but they're far in the past, and spring is far in the future, and if you feel like feeling lousy, well, you've got a reason.

It was just that kind of day in Concord on January 28, 1986, with an overcast sky and a thermometer that had bottomed out at fourteen degrees. But it was hard to find so much as a single person feeling any gloom, and that was especially true in all of the city's schools. Few of the students were going to be doing much work today, at least not in the morning. What they'd be doing instead was watching television. All over Concord, TVs had been set up in schools the day before so that they'd be ready to go first thing in the morning. Nowhere were the preparations greater than at Concord High School.

Dozens of TVs had been scattered everywhere in the building—in classrooms and hallways and in the library. There were some in the cafeteria, too, as well as in the auditorium, where as many students as could fit would be crowding in with noisemakers and signs and confetti and party hats. On a day as grand as this, attendance at Concord High would be almost perfect—the one exception, of course, being social studies teacher Christa McAuliffe.

The kids at Concord High had gotten used to Mrs. McAuliffe being away a lot that year—and she had a very good reason. The previous July, she'd been invited to the White House, where Vice President George H. W. Bush announced that she had been selected as the first private citizen to fly aboard the space shuttle. In 1984, President Ronald Reagan had announced that with four shuttles in America's fleet and with all of them having combined to fly twenty-four missions in just the past five years, it was time for a non-astronaut to share in the work—and in the adventure.

Reagan decided that that non-astronaut should be a teacher, since it would be awfully hard to think of someone who could better educate the nation about the science of space travel and the importance of the space program than someone for whom education was a lifetime mission. More than 11,000 teachers had applied for the chance to take the great flight. That number had been narrowed down to 114—two from every state and territory in the United States, as well as from Native American schools and overseas schools for the Departments of State and Defense. And that 114 had been narrowed to just ten.

Those ten were in the White House that day, when the vice president announced that of all of them, McAuliffe was the one who had most impressed the people at NASA with her enthusiasm and fitness and preparedness for flight, and so she would be the one who would get to make the trip. The runner-up was Barbara Morgan, a teacher from McCall, Idaho, who would train with McAuliffe and fly in her place if she somehow fell short—but nobody expected her to fall short. When the vice president made his announcement, all of the other finalists applauded McAuliffe—as finalists in such situations will do. And all of them hugged her—which finalists also do, even if the hugs hide a deep disappointment at having come so close to achieving something so remarkable and just missing out.

As the reporters crowded around her after the announcement, McAuliffe took care to be mindful of the feelings of the other nine contenders, promising to carry them in her thoughts on her way to space. "When that shuttle goes up, there might be one body, but there's going to be ten souls that I'm taking with me," she said.

Later, though, as she toured the country, appearing on talk shows and news shows that all wanted a moment of her time before she disappeared into training and then flew into history, she could allow herself to acknowledge her extraordinary good fortune. "If you're offered a seat on a rocket ship," she said, "don't ask what seat. Just get on."

Now, on January 28, that seat in that rocket ship, the

space shuttle *Challenger*, was waiting for her on the launchpad at Cape Canaveral in Florida. But there was reason to worry about whether any spacecraft had any business taking off from Florida that day. The punishing cold that had its hold on the country's northeast had crept down to seize the south, too, with parts of the Florida coast plummeting to just twenty-nine degrees. At Canaveral, where NASA's launchpads sat on a spit of land poking into the ocean, the miserable weather was leading to just the kind of miserable moods that the people in Concord had been spared.

An unaccustomed frost was on the windows of the vans and other vehicles parked out at the pads; the breath of the workers preparing the shuttle for launch condensed into thick, white vapor; and the space shuttle itself—a 184-foot tower of metal and glass and ceramic and rubber, filled with more than four million pounds of explosive fuel—was caked with heavy slabs of ice. Its wings, its joints, the scaffold-like launch tower that stood next to it, all were glittering with an Arctic-like covering. No shuttle had ever launched before in weather below fifty-four degrees; today's temperature was little more than half that.

Worse—much worse—the *Challenger* had a secret. It was a secret buried deep inside two of its engines, in spots where about two million of those four million pounds of fuel would soon be ignited. A few people knew the secret—people at NASA, people at the company that manufactured the engines—and they had worked hard to fix the problem that had been causing them all so much worry. This morning, as the televisions flicked on all over the nation, and the astronauts climbed into their bright orange space suits, the people at the Cape had convinced themselves that they'd indeed succeeded, that the space shuttle *Challenger* was fit to fly. But not everybody was so sure.

The year before, Bob Ebeling, one of the engineers at the manufacturing company, had written a memo to his superiors about the dangers of launching a shuttle in cold weather, and had titled the memo, simply, "Help!" But that stark alarm had not made an impression—or at least not a sufficient one—and the plans for the flight went on. The night before the launch, Ebeling saw the weather forecast for the next day and turned to his wife.

"It's going to blow up," he said simply. Then he tried, as best he could, to get a little sleep.

The space shuttle was supposed to be an exceedingly easy ship to fly. The idea behind it was straightforward enough—a spacecraft that could take off like a rocket and land like an airplane, with a giant cargo bay like the trunk of a car, allowing the ship to ferry satellites and other equipment to and from orbit quickly and cheaply. NASA expected there to be a lot of work for so practical a space truck, so the agency built four of them, each costing more than $1 billion. With a fleet that big, at least one of the shuttles should be flying all the time. When any one of them returned to Earth, it would be a simple matter of hosing it off, gassing it up, trotting out a fresh crew and sending the ship back aloft within a few days.

But things did not work out like that. Just because a vehicle looks like an airplane doesn't mean it's anywhere near as simple or reliable. It takes an enormous amount of energy to muscle a spacecraft off the ground and get it moving at an orbital speed of 17,500 miles per hour and an altitude of about 200 miles—or thirty times higher and thirty-one times faster than a passenger jet flies.

That kind of energy also requires an enormous amount of fuel, so while the shuttle itself measured 122 feet from nose to tail, it needed a giant, whalelike fuel tank—154 feet long—attached to its belly just to keep its engines fed all the way to orbit. And even that wouldn't provide enough liftoff oomph, so two comparatively slim engines, each 150 feet long, would have to be attached to the sides of the fuel tank.

The tank was designed to carry liquid fuel—supercold oxygen and hydrogen. The two additional engines would carry a solid fuel, similar in color and texture to a pencil eraser. The liquid-fueled engines could be throttled up and down or shut off entirely, more or less the same way the engine of a gasoline-fueled car can. The solid-fuel engines were another matter: once they were lit, there was no way to turn them off until they'd burned through all of that rubbery fuel. And they would burn hot—reaching 5,000 degrees, or half the tempera-ture of the surface of the sun. The solid engines and the fuel tank would operate only for the first ten minutes of the flight, after which they would be jettisoned and fall back into the ocean, while the shuttle and the crew flew on to orbit.

But a lot of damage could be done in ten minutes if things went wrong—and that was where the shuttle's dark secret lay. The solid rocket engines were composed of five cylinder-shaped segments—each of them like a giant tin can without a top or bottom—stacked and welded together and then filled with fuel. To make sure the seams where the segments connected couldn't leak, each one was sealed with something called an O-ring, a rubbery doughnut that circled the inside of the engine casing, covering up the seam. The O-rings were flexible, able to expand and contract slightly to seal even the tiniest gap in the seam. But when it was cold outside, the rings could lose their flexibility and grow brittle instead. And when they grew brittle, the fire could escape. That was what had worried Bob Ebeling and all of the other engineers who had looked at the thermometer and seen the ice hanging from the shuttle.

Still, if anything seemed like a good-luck ship— one that could shake off a little trouble on the launchpad before soaring successfully to space—it was *Challenger*. It had flown nine of the twenty-four shuttle missions so far, making it, at that point, the true workhorse of the fleet. And today, *Challenger* would be flying with an especially good crew, one with a lot of experience.

The commander was Dick Scobee, a shuttle veteran who had flown once before, in 1984. The pilot was Mike Smith—a shuttle rookie but a man who had graduated from the Naval Academy and served as a pilot in the Vietnam War. Also on board were Ellison Onizuka, Judith Resnik and Ronald McNair, all of whom, like Scobee, were flying their second mission; along with Gregory Jarvis, an air force engineer, who, like McAuliffe and Smith, was a rookie. Scobee and Smith were seated in the shuttle's cockpit during liftoff; the other five astronauts were seated one deck below.

A good ship and a solid crew, however, were no guarantee

against launch delays due either to weather or mechanical problems, and the *Challenger* had had plenty of them. The mission was originally set to begin on January 22; then it was the 23rd, and then the 24th, and then the 25th and then the 27th. And every single time, something got in the way.

On the morning of the 28th, though, the sky was clear, the ship seemed sound, and as long as you tried not to notice the huge chunks of ice all over a shuttle that was never, ever supposed to fly that way, it seemed like a lovely morning for a liftoff. The viewing stands for dignitaries, celebrities and the families of the astronauts were fuller than usual that day, with the teacher who was about to become a space traveler drawing media attention from around the world.

McAuliffe's husband, Steven, and their children, Caroline, six, and Scott, nine, were spared the crush of the reporters and were allowed to watch the launch with NASA personnel from the roof of the nearby launch control building. From there, Scott could look down and see twenty members of his third-grade class, who had traveled from Concord with their teacher and a few parents and were given seats in the viewing stands; for this day, at least, they were celebrities, too.

The astronauts had awakened early that morning, had a final medical exam and a group breakfast and then left the crew building for the ceremonial walk out to the van that would take them to the launchpad for their 9:38 a.m. liftoff. The distance from the door of the building to the door of the van was little more than a couple of dozen steps, but it would be the last chance for most of the people staying behind on Earth to see the crew before they flew to space. For that reason, the press was gathered here, too, shouting questions and taking pictures in the few seconds they had. The crew smiled and waved and then, one by one, climbed into the back of the van.

It was a relief when the last of them was inside, the door was closed and they could collect themselves in the sudden quiet. Johnny Corlew, a technician who was escorting them to the pad, knew enough not to bother astronauts in a moment like this, but he had a word of warning for them. Pointing to the tiny bathroom in the van, he told them that if any of them felt the urge, this would be their last chance, since the pipes in the bathroom at the top of the launch tower had frozen.

"It's pretty cold to be flying today," he said, almost apologetically.

"No, it's great weather to be flying in," Scobee, the commander, answered. "Nice and clear."

When the crew reached the launchpad and rode up the elevator to the top of the spacecraft, McAuliffe—though a low-ranking member of the crew compared to Scobee and Smith—remained a celebrity. The launchpad workers had sent pilots and scientists and engineers to space before, but never a teacher. The day before, when the crew had shown up for yet another planned launch that was scrubbed, one of the technicians had greeted McAuliffe wearing a graduation hat and a tassel. Today, Corlew tried to match that: just before McAuliffe entered the spacecraft, he produced an apple for the teacher and presented it to her with a smile and a flourish.

McAuliffe laughed, but with her hands in gloves and her

helmet under her arm, she could hardly take it now. "Save it for me," she said. "I'll eat it when I get back."

Corlew promised he would.

Once strapped into their seats, the crew would have to wait through yet another two-hour delay, pushing their planned launch from 9:38 to 11:38. The extra time was needed partly to fix some minor technical problems, and partly to give the sun time to rise a little higher, making things easier for the pad technicians who were laboring to chip the ice away.

Finally, the countdown resumed and the hundreds of people in the viewing stands quieted themselves and turned their attention to the sight of the rocket on the pad. The millions of people in the classrooms and school auditoriums and homes and offices who were watching the launch did the same, as did the three people on the roof of the launch control building who had the same last name as the teacher in the seat on the shuttle's lower deck.

The countdown rolled from three minutes down to two and then, at one minute and forty-six seconds, a mechanical arm with a small cap at its end, which was attached to the top of the external fuel tank to control escaping gas, disconnected and began to retract as it was supposed to. Through his window, Scobee could see the arm moving.

"There goes the beanie cap," he said.

Onizuka, who could also see it, responded teasingly: "Doesn't it go the other way?" Shuttle crews didn't usually make jokes this close to ignition, but after so many delays, the Challenger crew was feeling playful.

"God, I hope not, Ellison," said Smith, playing along.

Resnik got them back to business. "Got your harnesses locked?" she asked, reminding them that when the engines lit they'd all feel a kick and they'd best have their seat restraints clicked and tightened.

With the countdown clock now at just one minute until ignition, the noisy students at Concord High School grew still. In the classroom of teacher Susan Capano, which usually seated thirty students, at least sixty kids and eight teachers had gathered to watch the TV in the front of the room. In the cafeteria, where not only students but television news crews had gathered, the TV cameras were focused on the students, watching them as intently as they were watching the TVs. For audiences around the country, the reactions of the kids would be almost as exciting as the sight of the launch. In the auditorium, the noisemakers had stopped blasting, and the signs had been lowered. At the moment of ignition, the happy pandemonium would erupt once more all over the school, and the TV cameras would have plenty of happy kids to show the country.

At last, the clock reached zero. As it did, the liquid fuel in the giant external tank began to flow into the spacecraft, and the *Challenger*'s main engines lit. At the same time, the solid-fuel engines on either side of the tank came to life, too. A brilliant, sun-like light, almost too bright to look at directly, streamed and bloomed from the bottom of the spacecraft, and a great, roaring noise rolled out in all directions—a sound so deep and resonant that it was felt as much as heard. It rolled over the happy celebrities in the viewing stands, across the entire

Canaveral grounds and out to Highway A1A nearby. It rolled, too, over the father and the two young children standing on the roof of the launch control building.

"Liftoff!" called the Canaveral public affairs officer. "Liftoff on the twenty-fifth space shuttle mission, and it has cleared the tower."

At Concord High, the expected eruption of cheers and noisemakers and jumping and hugging happened on cue and seemed to shake the entire building. In schools across the country, similarly giddy scenes played out. In the spacecraft, things remained businesslike. *Challenger* climbed steadily higher and its velocity grew steadily greater, reaching an altitude of three miles and a speed of 1,500 miles per hour, and then tearing past that.

"Going through nineteen thousand," Scobee said, calling out the altitude, in feet.

"Throttle up," Smith said, as the liquid engines accelerated.

"Roger, go at throttle up," Scobee confirmed.

On CNN, the broadcaster, Tom Mintier, like the rest of the millions watching the launch, sounded relieved. "So the twenty-fifth mission of the space shuttle is now under way, after more delays than NASA cares to count," he said.

Then, unheard by Mintier, unheard by the TV audience, unheard by almost anybody, one more transmission came down from the spacecraft. It was from Smith, in the right-hand seat of the cockpit, and what he said was: "Uh-oh."

What Smith didn't know until that instant—and what he suddenly did know as the instruments in front of him sounded all manner of alarms—was that the *Challenger* had at last been pushed too hard. At the bottom of the right-hand solid fuel engine, one of the O-rings had failed precisely as feared. Within seconds after liftoff, a small white flame had broken through that engine's casing, directly adjacent to the gigantic external fuel tank, which was filled with 390,000 gallons of explosive liquid hydrogen. The little flame burned and burned like a finely focused torch, training its destructive power on a single spot on the aft portion of the tank. Finally, at the seventy-third second of the mission, it burned all the way through the wall of the tank, instantly igniting the hydrogen, which erupted in a massive explosion. In an eyeblink, the tank vanished entirely, replaced by a giant white cloud of vapor and debris. The solid rocket boosters, which were suddenly unmoored from the tank and could not stop burning their fuel until it was all gone, flew on mindlessly. From the ground, all that was visible was a two-fingered fireball high overhead.

"Looks like a couple of the solid rocket boosters blew away from the side of the shuttle," a confused Mintier said on CNN.

In Mission Control, Steve Nesbitt, the public affairs officer who, along with the network newscasters, narrated the mission for the TV audience, was focusing not on a TV screen, but on the monitor screen in the console in front of him, which was filled with a stream of data reporting the state of the spacecraft. So far, everything looked fine. A navy flight surgeon sitting to his left, however, saw the picture of the explosion on a nearby TV and asked in alarm, "What was that?"

Nesbitt snapped his head to the TV, saw what the flight

surgeon had seen, then turned back to his own screen and saw something that in some ways was even more awful. All of the data—all of the numbers and letters that were the vital signs of a healthy spacecraft—had vanished. In their place was nothing but an unbroken series of "M"s—for *missing*.

Nesbitt knew he had to say something, anything at all; it was his job to explain things, after all. But he had no explanation to offer, so he went with the only thing he could say knowledgeably and irrefutably.

"Flight controllers are looking very carefully at the situation," he said. "Obviously a major malfunction."

In the balcony of the auditorium at Concord High School, where the celebration was still under way, someone shouted, "Shut up, everyone!"

In the cafeteria, a teacher jumped up on a table and echoed that. "Everybody shut up! Something's wrong!"

In her classroom, Capano silenced the sixty students and eight teachers, and at that moment, they heard a commentator on TV flatly announce, "The vehicle has exploded."

"What do they mean 'the vehicle'?" a girl in the class asked her.

"I think they mean the shuttle," Capano answered.

"No, no, no!" the girl cried. "They don't mean the shuttle! They don't mean the shuttle!"

On the ground at Cape Canaveral, where reporters stood in a group, squinting up at the sky, someone asked, "Where are they?"

Another reporter, one who had covered multiple shuttle

liftoffs before and knew what a good launch looked like and what a disaster looked like, answered succinctly: "Dead," he said. "We've lost 'em. God bless 'em."

He was not quite right—at least not yet. When the tank exploded and the solid boosters flew off, the shuttle was left briefly suspended in space, largely intact but with no functioning engines. As it began to fall, however, plunging toward the ocean below at over 200 miles per hour, the force of the air against the body of the ship began to rip it apart. Tail, fins, wings, hull, all tore free and pinwheeled off. All that was left intact was the sturdiest part of the ship, which was the airtight compartment that housed the cockpit, the belowdeck and all seven astronauts.

No one knows how long the crew of the space shuttle *Challenger* survived—no one will ever know—but the compartment did not hit the water until after about two minutes and forty-five seconds of free fall. When the wreckage was eventually recovered from the bottom of the ocean, at least four of the astronauts' emergency oxygen kits had been opened up and activated, which probably meant that they were alive at least long enough to realize what was happening and to begin the survival drills they had practiced. On the instrument panel, switches were positioned in a way that indicated that Scobee and Smith were desperately doing whatever they could to restore power and regain some kind of control over whatever was left of their ship—but there was, effectively, no ship left at all, and with communications to the ground severed, the astronauts were entirely alone.

Astronaut Robert Overmyer, who knew Scobee well and even owned a plane with him, is confident of how his friend conducted himself in what would prove to be the last seconds of his life. "I know Scob did everything he could to save his crew," Overmyer said. "He flew that ship without wings all the way down."

There would, however, have been nothing even the best pilot could do. The *Challenger* crew struck the ocean at 208 miles per hour and any of them who were still alive would have died on impact at about the same moment that, had the mission progressed as it was supposed to, they would have arrived in orbit. At the Cape, the horrified dignitaries, guests and family members—including the three McAuliffes on top of the launch control building—were ushered hurriedly away and loaded onto buses, which would drive them back to buildings far from the launchpad at Cape Canaveral. There, the terrible details would be explained to them.

The astronauts' remains would be recovered from the crew compartment and given proper burials. Much of the shuttle debris would be recovered, too. That wreckage would be useful in the long investigation that would follow, with a government commission that included Neil Armstrong, the first man on the moon, and Chuck Yeager, the first person to fly a plane faster than the speed of sound, analyzing how things could have gone so horribly wrong. Eventually, they would lay the blame on a great many things, including pressure from the government to launch shuttles as quickly as possible, and a refusal by manufacturers and NASA to listen to the concerns of engineers like

Bob Ebeling, who had written the memo with the desperate word "Help!" Blame would also be laid on the cursed O-rings.

The rings would be modified to make a future burn-through less likely. New rules would be imposed forbidding cold-weather launches; other rules would slow down production of parts that presented a danger and empower engineers and workers to bring all of the work to a halt if the conditions weren't safe. And then, as must happen after a tragedy, the country and the world would move on.

Americans would return to space in September of 1988, when the shuttle *Discovery* would be launched on a four-day mission. Steven McAuliffe, who became a widower at the hands of cold weather and bad machinery, would eventually remarry. Much later, his two children would follow their mother's example and become teachers. As the anniversaries rolled by, none of the McAuliffes especially liked to talk to the press about the terrible day in the bitter cold when their family and the nation experienced such devastation. On February 1, 2003, however, the nation would have to live through the same horror over again, when the shuttle *Columbia* broke apart on reentry, killing seven crew members just as *Challenger* had. Ultimately, the shuttles would quit flying for good in the summer of 2011, with the last flight of the shuttle *Atlantis*.

On the evening of January 28, 1986, however, the first of the twin shuttle horrors was still fresh. President Reagan, who had planned to make his annual State of the Union address to Congress that night, instead postponed his long, formal speech and replaced it with a much shorter, much more intimate talk to the nation. Sitting in the White House, he spoke into the camera about the terrible loss America had suffered, and offered his sympathy to the astronauts' families. He also took special care to add a few words for the schoolchildren who were watching.

"I know it is hard to understand," he said, "but sometimes painful things like this happen. It's all part of the process of exploration and discovery. The *Challenger* crew was pulling us into the future, and we'll continue to follow them."

Schoolchildren surely took comfort from that. But the sweet genius of the sentiment was that a lot of the adults watching that evening probably did as well. Even now, years on, many still do.

NASA's shuttle Atlantis *docked with Russia's* Mir *space station. "Mir" means peace, but not every day in the life of the old station would earn that name.*

> ELEVEN >

CRACK-UP IN ORBIT

Mir Space Station, 1997

IT CAN BE oddly peaceful inside a dying spacecraft. That was not something Michael Foale ever suspected—and with good reason. When you're inside a spacecraft that's dying, you're likely to die right along with it. But now that Foale was in that very situation, he was surprised at the sense of serenity that came over him.

Foale had been aboard Russia's *Mir* space station for six weeks, ever since the American space shuttle *Atlantis* carried him aloft on May 15, 1997. In that time, he'd gotten used to the constant whir of the fans and churning of the pumps and the low buzz of the electrical systems that serve as the soundtrack for life in space. Then, too, there was the fluorescent wash of blue-white lights that made it forever daytime inside the ship.

But when the power shuts down, everything goes quiet and dark. The only available source of light is the view of the Earth

200 miles below, popping into vivid relief in the windows. It was a magnificent sight, and if that turned out to be the last sight you ever saw, well, there were worse ways to go.

Foale had no intention of looking his last on the world that night, though—not if he had anything to say about it. The problem was, he might not have anything to say about it. Nor might his two crewmates, Russian cosmonauts Aleksandr Lazutkin and Vasily Tsibliyev.

The *Mir* space station had spent eleven years orbiting the Earth, since 1986, and it was not news to anybody that it was falling apart fast. Power, oxygen, electrical systems and more were forever breaking down and requiring patchwork repairs, many of the fixes invented on the fly since the replacement parts that had always been available under the generous state funding of the old Soviet system were no longer so quick in coming in the new, ramshackle Russian economy. The result was that the *Mir* spacecraft—the quarter-million-pound, hundred-foot-long crown jewel of the country's space program—was fast going ramshackle, too.

This morning, it seemed like the end might finally have come, after a devastating accident that crippled the space station, breached its hull, sent its atmosphere bleeding away and knocked the station into a slow, powerless tumble from which, for now at least, there appeared to be no recovering.

That was the mess Foale and Lazutkin and Tsibliyev found themselves in as they sat together in the central module of the *Mir*, hunkered down behind closed hatches to preserve the air they had left, waving flight plans in front of their faces to fan away the carbon dioxide they were exhaling and hoping some oxygen—with no fans to circulate it—would flow in to replace it.

Mission Control in Houston, they knew, could not help them. Mission Control in Moscow could send up advice and ideas, but it would be up to the crew themselves to fix the *Mir* or they'd die along with it, and that endgame would play out soon. The peace and quiet and beautiful view outside the window did nothing to change that hard reality.

NASA astronauts aboard the *Mir* space station were never under the illusion that they would serve as anything more than the very lowest-ranking member of a three-person team, and Foale had been aware of that reality from the start. Russia had its rules about who would fly the ships, who would give the orders and who would obey those orders, and all the top jobs would go to Russians.

Even if the two higher-ranking crew members wanted to share the load with the lowest, there were compelling reasons not to. The newly capitalist Russia included bonuses and other incentives in the cosmonauts' flight contracts: the more work you do in space, the more rubles you get when you return to Earth.

So Foale accepted his lowly role, and for the past six weeks had left the truly hard stuff to Tsibliyev and Lazutkin, contributing mostly to the scientific experiments conducted aboard the station. On the evening of June 24, however, he knew that the next day the entire crew would be working as one, taking on what was easily the hardest job they'd faced in space so far.

Every few months, an uncrewed cargo vessel called the *Progress* would be sent to the *Mir* with fresh supplies. Docking the eight-ton, twenty-three-foot *Progress* with the station should be a relatively routine maneuver, with the commander, Tsibliyev for this rotation, flying the cargo vessel by remote control throughout most of its approach, an exercise he'd practiced uncounted times on the ground.

Things were usually made even easier by the fact that the final 100 yards of the approach, known as the red zone, would be handled by an automatic guidance system, which did not rely on the less precise eyeball reckoning that a human pilot would have to use. That was good because the red zone could easily become a kill zone if the *Progress* went awry.

Now, however, the automatic system would not be part of the process. Ukraine, which had recently broken away from Russia, was home to the guidance radars and, having tasted the fruits of capitalism and liked them as much as the Russians did, had begun overcharging for its services. It was a price Moscow refused to pay.

The result was that Tsibliyev would have the job of steering the *Progress* vessel the entire way in. Even for a cool-handed, stick-and-rudder pilot like him, that wouldn't be easy. From his command station in the main module, there was a window he could use to see the *Progress* as it drew near, but given the angle of the approach, the ship wouldn't appear within the frame until the very last part of the maneuver.

Instead, a TV camera on the *Progress* vessel would be trained on the *Mir* itself and beam that image to a TV monitor mounted on the station's main instrument panel. Tsibliyev would essentially be flying in reverse—watching his own vessel grow larger as the smaller ship approached, until he finally brought the *Progress* in for a docking. A few months before, when another crew was trying a similar maneuver, the TV camera had temporarily failed, leaving that commander briefly flying entirely blind.

All of that was much on Tsibliyev's mind on the evening of June 24, as the three men sat at the small table in the main module, eating a rare Western-style beef stew dinner—a pleasant break for Foale from the warm borscht and jellied perch that were so often on the menu. Outside, somewhere far away in the dark, the *Progress* vehicle was already parked in orbit, waiting for the commander to bring it in.

Tsibliyev picked at his food and turned worriedly to Lazutkin. "This is a bad business, Sasha," he said, using the Russian nickname for Aleksandr. He did not have to specify what that bad business was.

"It's all right, Vasily," Lazutkin answered. "The engineers need this, and you can do it."

Tsibliyev shook his head in a slow no. "It's bad," he said. "It's a dangerous thing to do."

The next morning, whatever dark spirits had taken hold of Tsibliyev had apparently vanished. Even before Foale opened his eyes, he could hear a tape of Russian romantic music playing from the direction of Tsibliyev's sleep station. The commander always played romantic music when he was in a good mood.

When Tsibliyev floated into the main module, Foale could see that he had even dressed for the role of a man in command. Instead of his usual, rumpled jumpsuit, he had put on the stiffer, scratchier one he would use for pictures or for welcome days, when a new crew arrived. He had a pilot's work to do today, and he would look the part.

Lazutkin floated into the central module and began running the cables to hook up the television monitor. Tsibliyev and Foale eyed the dark TV screen warily. Lazutkin noticed and smiled.

"You're not going to have a problem this time," he assured Tsibliyev. "The picture is not going to disappear."

The cosmonauts mostly spoke Russian to each other, and Foale understood some of it. When they spoke to Foale, they switched to English, and he offered his own bits of Russian when he responded. In this cooperative if imperfect way, they could make themselves understood.

When the system was ready, Lazutkin switched it on and the monitor flickered to life, showing mostly the blackness of space and a part of the curve of the Earth below. Lazutkin seemed pleased; Foale knew he should be, too—but he wasn't.

The *Mir* station was supposed to be visible in the middle of the frame, and it was, more or less. *Progress* was approaching from above, so the image showed the giant station as a small, dark spot against the cloud cover below. If Tsibliyev was going to bring the distant *Progress* safely into the *Mir*'s docking port, he would have to do a lot of deft flying.

Straightaway, Tsibliyev took hold of the two joysticks on the panel in front of him and began to go to work.

The *Mir* began to grow on the screen, and Foale felt a bit more confident. Tsibliyev took one hand from one of the sticks, picked up a stopwatch and began glancing at the seconds, timing how fast the station's solar panels—its biggest and most conspicuous features—appeared to be growing. Too slow was a waste of time; too fast would be dangerous.

Foale said nothing. Tsibliyev looked untroubled, and that was all the American needed to see.

But then, a moment later, Tsibliyev's expression changed. Foale glanced at the range finder on the instrument panel readouts; the *Progress* was about 3,500 feet away. He glanced at the TV screen. The solar panels were growing way too rapidly.

Tsibliyev hit one of the joysticks hard—in the direction that would slow the cargo ship down. The solar panels on the *Mir* kept growing at the same speed.

Tsibliyev hit his sticks again. The speed did not change; if anything, it increased.

"Michael, try getting a range mark," Tsibliyev ordered.

Foale pushed off of a bulkhead and shot into the adjacent Kvant module—a small lab and work space. He peered out the window, but the *Progress* was not yet in frame.

"Nothing," he called ahead of himself as he swam back into the main module.

"Sasha?" Tsibliyev asked, as Lazutkin peered through his porthole in the main module.

"Nothing," Lazutkin answered.

On Tsibliyev's TV monitor, the space station got bigger and bigger as the *Progress* closed from 3,000 to 2,000 to 1,000 feet and kept coming. When the range indicator read just 150 feet, the station's solar panels practically blotted out the entire screen.

"Try to get another range!" Tsibliyev shouted at both of the other men.

Foale headed back for the Kvant, but before he even reached the passageway between modules, Lazutkin looked out his window and called, "There it is already! It's coming in—fast!"

Then Tsibliyev barked out the order that Foale was hoping not to hear. "Michael! Get in the spacecraft!" he said.

"The spacecraft," in this case, meant the *Soyuz* vehicle that was always kept attached to the station and that could be used as a lifeboat and a ride home in case of an emergency. An order to get inside it meant, *power it up and prepare it for flight because we may need to abandon ship.*

Foale dashed through the opposite hatch into what was known as the transfer node—a spherical structure with six different portholes to which six different modules were docked.

The second he got there, he heard and felt a powerful bang and jolt. Instantly, a horn began to sound.

The *Mir* had been hit—and hit hard.

Foale knew what the rules called for him to do now, and

that was to stay absolutely still and pay attention to the feeling inside his head. If he felt nothing, the spacecraft was intact. If he felt a mild popping in his ears, it meant that somewhere along its breadth, the *Mir*'s hull had been breached, and it was leaking air. If he felt a sudden, extremely painful popping, it could well be the last thing he'd feel, because it would mean that the space station had been ripped wide open.

He felt the subtler pop. The *Mir* was seriously wounded, but there was time.

Foale turned to the hatch that led to the *Soyuz* and was alarmed to see that a tangle of cables lay in his path—perhaps knocked free by the collision. Whatever the cause, it meant trouble.

He began clearing the cables away, and as he did, he saw Lazutkin appear beside him, fighting with more cables at a different hatch, the one that led to the Spektr module, which served as living quarters and storage area.

"I saw it hit," Lazutkin said before Foale could ask. "It was Spektr."

Spektr, Lazutkin was telling him, was where the breach was. Even as Foale was fighting to open the closed hatch that led to the *Soyuz*, Lazutkin was working to close the opened one that led to Spektr, sealing off the module and the leak along with it.

In short order they had those twin jobs done. The space station was stable for the moment, but it wouldn't stay that way for long.

Foale and Lazutkin floated back to the main module, met

Tsibliyev there and began to review their circumstances and the limited options they had to save both their spacecraft and themselves.

The *Progress* vehicle was not a concern anymore. Its whereabouts were unknown, but wherever it was, it was out of the way, and that was good. It had done its damage, however.

Not only had it punched a hole in the *Mir*; it had also knocked the entire station into a slow roll, which spelled trouble in a number of ways.

The station got its power from the solar panels, keeping the systems running when the *Mir* was on the daytime side of the Earth and recharging the batteries, which could run down fast, and would be needed for the passage over the nighttime side. A rolling spacecraft, however, could not point the panels to the sun, and already anything on the *Mir* that relied on electricity—which meant everything, including the vital life-support systems—was flickering and failing.

Even that minimal power was possible only because the panels sometimes got lucky and caught a flash of sunlight as they rolled. On the dark side of the planet, there would be no power at all.

Stopping the roll would normally be easy, thanks to a series of thrusters arrayed around the exterior of the station. But those thrusters required electricity, too, and without any, they were useless.

More troubling still was the matter of the *Soyuz*, the crew's only way off this sinking ship. The *Soyuz* ran on its own internal power, but through an unfortunate trick of the wiring plan that no one had ever considered until now, turning on that power required the *Soyuz* to draw a little juice first from the *Mir*—and the *Mir* had none to give. A lifeboat you couldn't deploy would do you no good at all.

Before the crew could figure out if it was possible to stabilize the station, they had to know the rate of spin. A roll of, say, two revolutions per minute would be a lot harder to bring to heel than a roll of one or less. And no sooner had the three men begun to have that discussion among themselves than the ground jumped in and pressed them for answers.

"How fast are you rolling?" the capsule communicator called up from Moscow.

Tsibliyev, more out of reflex than anything else, looked down at his blacked-out instrument panel and shrugged. "We don't know," he answered.

But Foale had a way to figure it out. During his astronaut training, he had specialized in spacecraft guidance, and as any good navigator knows, there are fancy ways to steer a ship and very unfancy ones. He floated to a porthole, placed his thumb against the glass and watched how long it took stars to disappear behind it and then reappear. Then he did some mental math. He called back to Lazutkin: "Tell them we're moving one degree per second."

The message was relayed down and Moscow paused, clearly unpersuaded by such a rough job of ciphering. An impatient Lazutkin spoke up. "Yes," he said flatly. "Yes. Mike's right."

That was good news. One degree per second was extremely slow—enough that it could be stopped without the space station's thrusters at all. If one of the crew members hightailed it to the *Soyuz* and waited until the random drift of the station put the solar panels in position to pick up a flicker of sunlight, enough energy might be produced to bring the *Soyuz*'s systems online. Then the little lifeboat's thrusters might be able to stabilize the entire *Mir* structure. It wouldn't be easy—like a motor scooter pushing a bus—but it was possible.

It would be up to Tsibliyev, as the commander, to do the driving. Vanishing into the *Soyuz*, he waited for a well-aimed sunbeam and got one. Quickly, he flicked on the ship's guidance and engaged the thrusters. Then he called out that he was ready.

Foale and Lazutkin watched the stars at the windows and estimated the thruster bursts that would be needed.

"Okay, do three seconds!" Foale called to Tsibliyev.

The thrusters popped briefly and, in response, the ship bumped, but it was nowhere near a three-second firing. Foale looked at Lazutkin and both men knew what the problem was: the commander, whose responsibility it was to save this drifting hulk, was worried about making things worse by wasting fuel.

"Vasily, did you do it for real?" Foale called out.

"No, no, I didn't," Tsibliyev confessed. "I just did a blip."

Foale, humble rank or not, knew it was no time to be shy about speaking frankly to the boss.

"Vasily, we can't do this," he said. "We can't measure this thing unless you do it for the time we say. We've got to know how long you've done it so we can get rid of that motion."

Tsibliyev responded with a simple, "Okay," and gave the thrusters a three-second burst.

For the next few hours, Foale and Lazutkin called for more thruster bursts—four seconds here, two seconds there—and slowly, the crew took control of their broken ship, damping out the last of its unwanted roll and bringing the solar panels into the full light of the sun. All across the *Mir*, instrument panels flickered on, interior fans began to whir, pumps and radiators and guidance systems came back to life.

Finally, at just past midnight, or fourteen hours after an out-of-control *Progress* vehicle had done its damage, the *Mir* was back in service, and the crisis appeared to have passed.

It would be weeks before the *Mir* space station would be fully repaired. As quickly as possible, Russia sent up another *Progress* vessel—and paid Ukraine the needed money to dock it safely this time. On board was a hurriedly built adapter that would seal the breach in the broken Spektr module. Foale camped out in the *Soyuz* while his crewmates donned space suits and performed the repairs in the airless Spektr.

The crew flew together for two more months and then, in August, Tsibliyev and Lazutkin completed their shifts and went home. Foale followed two months after that, returning to Earth the same way he had left it, aboard a NASA shuttle.

Five more crews would rotate into and out of the space station over the next three years, with the last ones ending their stay in June of 2000.

After that, the tired *Mir* flew on alone, until, on March 21,

2001, timed firings of the engine of yet another attached *Progress* vehicle slowed its orbit and led it to a controlled, if fiery, plunge into the Pacific waters east of Australia and New Zealand.

By then, the much larger, much more capable *International Space Station* was being assembled. *Progress* cargo vehicles continue to resupply that station, too. But the hand-docking proved to be too difficult and too prone to breakdowns, and no cosmonaut or astronaut has ever been asked to bring a *Progress* in that way again.

This chapter was adapted from the author's previous work in *Time* magazine.

Italian astronaut Luca Parmitano trains for his spacewalk at NASA's weightlessness simulation pool in Houston. Water, Parmitano would later learn, is much better on the outside of a spacesuit than the inside.

> TWELVE >

THE ASTRONAUT WHO ALMOST DROWNED IN SPACE

International Space Station, 2013

SPACE HAS A lot of ways to kill you. It's a beautiful place to contemplate and a thrilling place to visit, but for all its appeal, it's got death in its heart.

Every astronaut who's ventured into space has been well acquainted with the dangers it offers up: death by radiation, death by asphyxiation, death by cold, death by heat, death during liftoff, death during reentry, death by collision, death by solar storm, death merely by wandering off course and getting swallowed up by space's limitless reach forever and ever and ever.

There is almost no way you can imagine to die that space won't be perfectly happy to deliver, save one: you can't drown there.

Earth is awash in water, and plenty of people have met their mortal ends as a result of that fact. Other worlds are equally wet: Jupiter's moon Europa has a deep, subsurface ocean—so does its sister moon Callisto and so does the dwarf planet Pluto. So, too, must an untold number of the thousands of exoplanets astronomers have discovered orbiting other stars.

But the small patches of space that humans have touched—the orbital regions around our planet and the plains of the nearby moon—are utterly dry.

That, ultimately, was what made it such a surprise in 2013 when Italian astronaut Luca Parmitano nearly drowned while orbiting 250 miles above the Earth.

It was a near-death the American, Russian and European space programs could have seen coming; indeed, it was a near-death they *should* have seen coming. A lot of people after the fact would say that Parmitano himself should have seen it coming, too.

Maybe that was true, but Parmitano was an astronaut, and he had a job to do. That day, July 16, 2013, the job included taking a space walk. There is no astronaut who's ever flown who would say no to a space walk. So Parmitano said yes, and out he went. And that, as it turned out, came very close to being the last decision he would ever make.

Luca Parmitano lived a charmed life. As a boy, he graduated from the prestigious State High School for Science in Catania, Italy, and went on to get an undergraduate degree in political science at the University of Naples, then a science degree at the Italian Academy of Aeronautics, and yet another degree in experimental flight test engineering at the Institute of Aeronautics and Space in Toulouse.

In 2001, he became an officer in the Italian Air Force and

excelled as both a squadron commander and test pilot. In 2009, he was selected by the European Space Agency to become an astronaut. And while other rookie astronauts sometimes waited half a decade or more for their first flight, by 2011 Parmitano was already training for his 2013 mission to the *International Space Station*. The station has been continuously occupied by different crews since the first one climbed aboard in 2000.

Parmitano was going to be among the station's first long-duration crew members, spending six months aloft conducting biomedical, astronomical and other scientific studies. He would also have the chance to float out on what were planned to be at least two space walks over the course of the six months.

On May 13, 2013, Parmitano's journey began, with a nighttime launch aboard a Russian *Soyuz* rocket from the Baikonur Cosmodrome in Kazakhstan. Since the Earth is always spinning and the space station is always orbiting, mission planners have to plan their liftoffs for the precise moment that the launchpad on the ground and the station up in space are in the right positions. And that sometimes means launching at night. Flying with Parmitano that evening were American astronaut Karen Nyberg and Russian cosmonaut and commander Fyodor Yurchikhin.

It took four orbits—or six hours—for the *Soyuz* to chase down the station. But at last, the three new arrivals docked and climbed aboard, where they were greeted by two more Russians, as well as by American astronaut Chris Cassidy, who would be Parmitano's partner on the two space walks.

There were a lot of items on the six-person crew's to-do list, but one of the most pressing was getting the already-huge station ready to grow bigger still. Russia's new, forty-three-foot-long laboratory module would be launched soon, and the station would have to be reconfigured to receive it, most urgently with new power and communications cabling that had to be strung along the station's structural truss—the girders and scaffolding that serve as its structural spine.

That was the principal reason for the two space walks—or EVAs, for extravehicular activity, as NASA referred to them. Parmitano and Cassidy's first excursion was set for July 9, and it would not be easy.

The walk was planned to last more than six hours—which meant a very long day of very physical labor that would begin hours before the astronauts actually stepped outside, with the slow, assisted business of suiting up and then at least 100 minutes of pre-breathing the backpack air to accustom the body to the suit environment.

Unlike most space suits, which are tailored exclusively to the astronaut who will wear them, EVA suits are simply too expensive and too complex to use once or twice and throw away. They are thus designed in less precise sizes to be used and reused by multiple crew members.

Parmitano would get the suit that was catalogued simply as number 3011, but the impersonally labeled garment could be personalized to its wearer at least a bit: when a NASA astronaut wore the suit, it would have an American flag on its shoulder, but that could be removed and replaced with other flags. Today, the suit would have the red, white and green flag of Italy.

After Parmitano and Cassidy were suited and ready, they were sealed inside the station's air lock, visible to the other crew members only through a porthole in the interior door. Slowly, the sea level air pressure of 14.7 pounds per square inch inside the air lock dropped to just .5 pounds, the point at which it was safe to open the outside hatch, allowing Parmitano and Cassidy to drift outside, connected to the station by safety tethers.

Parmitano was the second-ranked of the two spacewalkers, designated EV-2, but according to protocol, he would be the first out the door. He did not know precisely what to expect when he floated into the void, but what struck him first and most powerfully was the depth of the surrounding blackness.

On Earth, black is a color, the darkness you see when there is too little light to be reflected off the surrounding air. In space, black is an absence—a complete and consuming void as light streaks through a vacuum with no air anywhere to scatter it to the eye. The blackness of space is what *nothing* looks like.

Parmitano lingered to absorb what he was seeing—or not seeing—until Cassidy, who had taken three space walks on an earlier mission and was thus less taken by the view, floated out and nudged him from behind. Mindful of the time, he set them both to work.

The two spacewalkers' six hours outside would cover a bit more than four orbits. Half of each of those orbits would be spent on the daylight side of the Earth, where the station itself would be brightly illuminated even if the sky wasn't; the other half would be on the nighttime side, where they would have to rely on helmet lights to do their work.

The four orbits passed quickly and productively, and when the time was up, NASA ordered the astronauts to secure their work sites and go back inside.

Reentering the station could be as slow and painstaking as exiting it, but that job proceeded without incident except for one small problem that occurred in the air lock: when Parmitano removed his helmet, about a half a liter of water floated out.

That was a mystery. The two spacewalkers had faced each other, visor to visor, when they were reentering the station, and Cassidy had seen no water floating in his crewmate's helmet. It was possible it had been there anyway, pooling around the rubber dam in the suit just below Parmitano's neck, and that Cassidy had simply missed it.

The likelier explanation, however, was that the water had come from the drink bag that was built into the chest of the EVA suits, equipped with a straw that ran up into the helmet, so that the astronauts could stay hydrated during the hard, sweaty work. The repressurization of the air lock had likely compressed the bag, causing the water to leak up through the straw. Parmitano himself had probably made matters worse as he was bending forward to remove the helmet and crimped the bag further.

It was a small problem, one that could be easily prevented on the next walk if Parmitano drank the bag dry before reentering and then was careful about removing the suit. The astronauts reported the small anomaly to the ground and thought little more of it.

The second EVA took place exactly one week later. Again Parmitano drifted out first, and again Cassidy followed. This time, Parmitano—now a veteran, too—spent less time gazing about, and both men went straight to work. Parmitano headed aft to pick up the work he'd been doing a week earlier, and Cassidy headed fore.

That day, however, things would not go as smoothly as they had the last time. Barely thirty minutes into the six-hour walk, Parmitano was jolted by a carbon dioxide alarm sounding in his suit. At the same time, a corresponding indicator on the EVA director's console in Mission Control went off-scale high. The meaning of the dual alerts was ominous and unmistakable: Parmitano's life-support system had failed, his oxygen flow had shut down and he was about to choke to death on his own exhalations.

Except he wasn't. Despite the alarm, the oxygen indicators in his suit and on the ground showed no problem. The suit's power and circulation systems were functioning perfectly and, most important, his breathing was steady and relaxed, hardly the sign of a man who was dying of suffocation.

The CO_2 alert had to be mistaken—and it was quickly proven to be just that; within a minute, the alarm turned off and the readings on the Mission Control console returned to a healthy baseline. It was the kind of glitch that would occur if, say, a wire shorted out or an instrument got wet—a nuisance, perhaps, but nothing more.

No sooner had that problem resolved itself, however, than another, more troubling one surfaced: as Parmitano moved his head inside his suit, he noticed an unexpected dampness at the back of his neck. It was more than a dampness, actually; it seemed as if the rear collar of his inner garment was entirely soaked through.

That was not unusual when a spacewalker was working hard and breaking a heavy sweat. But sweat is body temperature, at least at first, and this water was cold. It was too cold even to be from the water bag, which hugged the body and stayed relatively warm. He moved his head again from side to side and felt a slight sloshing.

"I feel a lot of water on the back of my head, but I don't think it's from my bag," he informed Houston.

In Mission Control, the spacecraft communicator, astronaut Shane Kimbrough, frowned at the report.

"Luca," he called, "can you identify the source of the water?"

"I still feel it, and I cannot tell you the source," Parmitano answered.

If Parmitano couldn't identify what was causing the problem, the EVA controller in Mission Control believed he could, and he didn't like what he was thinking. He keyed open his mic to talk to the flight director.

"Flight," he said, "it could be coming from the vent port."

If that was so, it would be very bad news. The vent port was a small opening in the neck ring of the space suit that was supposed to allow excess humidity to escape harmlessly into the helmet. If it was leaking water instead, it meant that somewhere in the hundred yards of coolant tubing that ran through the suit there was a clog or a breach.

If so, once it began leaking it would simply continue, pouring a lot more water into the suit than a drink bag ever could—enough to flood it, in fact.

The flight director passed the EVA controller's assessment to Kimbrough and asked him to get a status check from Parmitano.

"Luca," Kimbrough called, "can you give us any good words on the water there? Is it increasing or decreasing?"

"It still feels the same," Parmitano answered. "It is not increasing nor decreasing."

Practically the moment Parmitano spoke those words, however, he felt a cold flow at the back of his neck. Worse, he felt the water migrating elsewhere in his helmet.

"It is increasing," he announced with greater urgency now. "It feels like a lot of water."

Cassidy, who had been monitoring the air-to-ground chatter, now shot over to Parmitano, took his crewmate's helmet in his hands and peered into his visor. He saw the water swirling around the neck of the suit.

"I see, I see it now. It's right there," he said, pointing to the base of the helmet. "Can you see it?"

Parmitano cast his eyes down as far as he could. "Yeah," he said. "It's about the same amount as when I took the helmet off last time, Chris."

"Really?" Cassidy asked worriedly. If Parmitano had half a liter of loose water in his suit after less than an hour outside, there was likely much more to come. Cassidy grasped at the last hopeful straw he could.

"It has to be the bag," he said, barely believing the words as he spoke them. "Can you suck it dry?"

Parmitano complied—and yet, if anything, the problem grew worse. Globules of water now clung to the interior of the visor, and Parmitano's forehead looked damp.

"It feels like sweat," Parmitano muttered. "How much can I sweat, though?"

Cassidy shook his head. "That stuff on your forehead isn't sweat," he said.

For a moment, Parmitano and Cassidy tried to continue their work as the ground controllers huddled to see if they could identify the problem and perhaps shut off whatever was causing the leak. If they stopped the flow entirely and if Parmitano felt comfortable enough, perhaps they could complete the EVA.

If anything, however, Parmitano was growing far less comfortable. The water level was undeniably increasing, and as it did, drops and blobs began drifting through the helmet, clinging to his exposed skin and raising the humidity inside the suit, which in turn caused his visor to cloud over. Worse, he began to notice that the foam-rubber covering of his earphones was becoming saturated and his communications link was crackling in and out.

"Chris," he called more urgently this time. "Chris, look at me. My head is really wet, and I have a feeling it is increasing."

Cassidy turned back to Parmitano. He saw what he estimated to be a full liter of water floating free in the helmet and informed the ground.

"Now it's in my eyes," Parmitano added.

In Houston, the EVA coordinator, who could hear everything the astronauts were saying, called to his support team over the Mission Control communications loop.

"Do we want to terminate?" he asked. Before he even got an answer, the flight director made the decision for him.

"Terminate EV-2," he ordered.

The command was succinct, and the key word—*terminate*—was deliberately chosen. In NASA-speak, the alternative to *terminate* was *abort*. Both meant essentially the same thing, but *abort* was intended to create a particular urgency and was saved for a true crisis, which this did not seem to be—so far.

Kimbrough heard the call and hailed the crew.

"Chris and Luca, based on what we've heard, we're going to terminate for EV-2. Chris, we'll get a plan up for you to clean things up and join him in a minute."

"Okay, copy all, Shane," Cassidy responded.

Parmitano nodded to Cassidy and turned to make his way back to the air lock—but it would not be easy. By now, his visor had become almost completely opaque, so much so that he had to move more by feel than by sight. As his vision failed, his hearing was going, too, with his headphones becoming wetter and his communications growing spottier.

Worse, there was now enough free-floating water in his helmet that it began obeying one of the curious laws of zero-g physics. With no downward pull of gravity, the droplets instead began clinging to his skin, and the capillary action caused them to form a thin film across his entire face—including his mouth and nose—like a sheet of plastic wrap he could not reach in to remove. He could drown just as easily wrapped in that layer as he could if the helmet were filled like a fishbowl.

Repeatedly, Parmitano shook his head to knock the water veil loose, then gasped in a quick breath before it collected again. As he groped his way along the station truss, he also gave his safety harness a yank. It had a recoil system similar to that of a window blind, designed to help reel an astronaut in automatically. The tug was a gentle one—just three pounds of force—but in the weightlessness of space it would help.

Even that, however, didn't work quite as planned. As the cable retracted, it spun Parmitano upside down. That disturbed the water that covered his face, forcing it into his nose and causing him to cough and choke. Then, gasping for breath and half-blinded by his visor, he suddenly became fully blinded as the space station sailed over to the nighttime side of the Earth and blacked out his field of view entirely.

Now Parmitano was well and truly cut off. He could move along only slowly and by touch. He strained to discern the distant, intermittent voices of Kimbrough and Cassidy in his saturated headphones and could make out something—faintly—but could not determine what they were saying.

There was, Parmitano knew, one more option if he could not find his way to the air lock before the suit became flooded entirely, but it was an option he did not want to try. His helmet was equipped with a depressurization vent, and if he opened it slightly, some of the water ought to stream out into space at least for a few seconds, before it froze solid and plugged the portal. That, however, could be just enough to free up his breathing and perhaps clear his visor, too. The problem was, he would have only one chance to get the venting right. If he mishandled the control, the depressurization would be sudden and complete and he would die in seconds.

That, he reckoned, was a risk he did not want to take, and he pressed on as best he could, fighting his way along the truss until he at last felt the rounded hull of what seemed to be the air lock. At that moment, a gap opened up in the curtain of water clinging to his visor, and his helmet lights fell on the thermal covering of the hatch, confirming that he was where he wanted to be.

Feeling around for the handle, he pulled it hard, swung the hatch open and fought his way inside.

"I'm at the air lock," he shouted out. "I've got a lot of water." His audio cut in and out badly, but Cassidy made out what he said.

"On my way, Luca," he called, abandoning his work and racing back to the open hatch.

When he reached it, he pushed inside behind Parmitano, who could not see him but could certainly feel the shove; vibrations in the hull also told him that Cassidy had sealed the hatch and hit the repressurization valve. With no radio link left between them at all now, they communicated by hand squeezes. Cassidy's said that he was here and was handling the repressurization; Parmitano's said that he was hanging on.

From the other side of the interior door, the rest of the crew, dressed in ordinary work clothes, watched through the porthole, waiting for the moment the pod was pressurized and they could burst through the door to help the two spacewalkers.

Parmitano counted off the seconds until that would happen, estimating how long it would take for the pressure to rise sufficiently high. He fought the impulse to throw off his helmet when the pressure was only halfway there. He might survive the sudden shock, but he would surely lose consciousness.

Finally, through the fog of his visor, he could make out a swirl of activity in front of him and could feel the shaking of the interior door opening. The other astronauts sprang toward him, twisted his helmet and threw it aside, and he gasped in the dry, abundant air around him. They helped him out of the top of his suit and dried his face with a towel.

Cassidy removed his helmet and beamed at Parmitano. "Luca's doing great," he informed the ground. "He's smiling and happy."

Both men knew that was only half-true. Parmitano was smiling, all right, but it was not the smile of a happy man. It was the smile of a shaken man who knew he had just gotten very lucky.

In the astronauts' formal summary to the ground, they would report that at least a liter and a half of water had floated out of Parmitano's helmet when they removed it, far more than the drink bag could ever have produced. The leak would ultimately be traced to contamination in a coolant filter in the suit, causing water to back up into the very vent port the ground had guessed was the problem.

Cleaning the filter helped, and suit 3011 would be certified for use again. As a precaution, however, both EVA suits would now also be equipped with snorkels running from the helmet down to the chest. In the event of a similar emergency, space-walkers would at least be able to breathe ambient suit air until they could get back inside.

Parmitano would go on to serve his full six-month rotation aboard the station, returning to Earth on November 11, 2013. He never flew or walked in space again, but his next career turn was all the same a fitting one: in 2014 he was selected as an aqua-naut, and spent two weeks the following year as commander of the *Aquarius* undersea lab off the coast of Key Largo in Florida. At no time in the days he spent living underwater did he ever face the danger of drowning.

› AUTHOR'S NOTE ›

THE GREAT JOURNEYS of the long-ago past, when adventurers in wooden ships set out to explore continents, were in some respects lost to history, since there were no reporters, news cameras or recording equipment around to capture the events as they unfolded. The great explorations of the twentieth and twenty-first centuries—when explorers set out in spacecraft— are another matter.

The stories told in *Disaster Strikes!* were reconstructed from many sources, most of which are publicly available. The most valuable among them was the Johnson Space Center History Office, an online resource that includes air-to-ground transcripts of most NASA missions since the very first American astronaut flew in 1961. All exchanges in the book between the spacecraft and the ground or between the astronauts themselves during flight were drawn from these transcripts and accompanying recordings. In some cases, the exchanges were edited or compressed for clarity and readability; in no event was the meaning or context changed.

All conversations for which there is no recording or transcript were reconstructed through interviews I conducted with the people involved, through their autobiographies, or with the help of NASA oral history interviews, which are also available on the NASA website. The history office also includes links to photos, diagrams and technical manuals. NASA's overall website—which connects to the sites of all of the space agency's various centers, including Cape Canaveral, the Jet Propulsion Laboratory and more—is also a valuable research tool.

An exceptional source for accounts of the missions as they happened is the *New York Times* online archives (called the *TimesMachine*), which includes reproductions of every page of every edition of the paper since the very first one published in 1851. Daily newspapers lack the long perspective of history, but they are rich in the details that give nonfiction narratives life.

Among the many books written by astronauts and flight controllers after they left NASA, the ones that were most valuable in my research were: *Countdown*, by Frank Borman; *The Last Man on the Moon*, by Eugene Cernan and Don Davis; *Carrying the Fire*, by Michael Collins; *Flight: My Life in Mission Control*, by Chris Kraft; *Failure Is Not an Option*, by Gene Kranz; and *Apollo EECOM: Journey of a Lifetime*, by Sy Liebergot.

Surprising insights into the old Soviet space program are available in the four-volume set *Rockets and People*, by Boris Chertok. The books are dense and detailed and not at all an easy read, but as a research resource, they are remarkable.

All of these sources, of course, are just a small portion of what is available—and what will become available in the future. The history of human space exploration is still being written—and recorded and photographed and filmed and more—and it is a history that will likely go on as long as humanity itself does. If the few chapters of that history we've lived in the last century and this one are any indication, there are remarkable stories to come.

> GLOSSARY >

AGENA: early unmanned spacecraft

APOLLO: three-person spacecraft designed to fly to the moon

ATTITUDE: the way the ship is pointed

BOOSTER: another word for a rocket

BURN: When a rocket's engines light, it is called a burn, because it is burning fuel.

CAPCOM: The person in Mission Control who radios up all information to the crew. The capcom is always an astronaut who is not flying on the current mission; the name is short for capsule communicator.

CAPE CANAVERAL: The launch site for spacecraft. For a time it was called Cape Kennedy.

COMMAND-SERVICE MODULE (CSM): The cone-shaped portion of the spacecraft that houses the crew is the command module; the astronauts and all the controls on their instrument panel command where the spaceship goes and what it does. The service portion is a cylindrical, twenty-four-foot structure attached to the rear of the command module like the trailer behind the cab of a truck. It contains the spacecraft's main engine, the SPS (service propulsion system), as well as much of its essential hardware, like oxygen tanks, water supply and batteries and fuel cells.

COSMONAUT: A Russian astronaut. (China calls its astronauts *taikonauts*.)

DROGUE: a small parachute that is used to slow down a returning spacecraft before its much-bigger main parachute is released

EECOM: The person in Mission Control responsible for the life-support systems in a spacecraft. The name stands for electrical, environmental and consumables manager, and in this case *consumables* refers to air, water, electricity and any other resources the astronauts use up during the mission.

EVA: A space walk. The initials stand for extravehicular activity—and *extravehicular* simply means "out of the vehicle."

EXTERNAL TANK: A gigantic orange fuel tank attached to the outside of the space shuttle that was actually larger than the shuttle itself. It was released and dropped back into the ocean shortly before the shuttle arrived in orbit.

FLIGHT DIRECTOR: the boss of Mission Control, responsible for all final decisions throughout a flight

FLIGHT DYNAMICS (FIDO): the Mission Control console operator who managed the trajectory, or route, of the rocket and the *Apollo* spacecraft

FLIGHT PLAN: a detailed plan of every moment of the mission and the roles of every player on the ground and in the air

GANTRY: A tall, movable, towerlike structure with a platform that supports the rocket and *Apollo* when they're on the launchpad. (Sometimes also referred to as a launch tower.)

GEMINI: two-person spacecraft designed for Earth orbit

INTERNATIONAL SPACE STATION (ISS): A space station that is currently in use. It was built by fifteen countries, led by the United States and Russia, and is the size of a football field.

JETTISON: let go or get rid of

LIQUID-FUELED ENGINE: a rocket engine that runs on liquid fuel, typically kerosene and supercold oxygen and hydrogen

LUNAR EXCURSION MODULE (LEM): A two-part ship. Its first task would be to land on the moon with its four legs and a powerful descent engine. When it was time to take off, the bottom half of the ship would serve as a launch platform, with explosive bolts and a guillotine system cutting the cables and other links to the top half, allowing an ascent engine to carry the remains of the spacecraft—which was essentially the crew cabin—up to lunar orbit.

MANNED: A mission that has humans aboard operating the craft. Today we say "crewed," since both men and women fly in space.

MERCURY: America's first crewed spacecraft, designed for one person

MIR: A Russian space station that was used from 1986 through 2001. It was smaller than the *International Space Station*.

MISSION CONTROL: The large auditorium-like room at the NASA space center in Houston where the space flight is managed. It houses consoles with experts who track and manage every technical aspect of the flight.

PITCH: when the nose of a spacecraft moves up or down; a 360-degree pitch would thus be a somersault

PROGRESS: The name of a Russian spacecraft that is used to deliver supplies to space stations. It is similar to the *Soyuz* but carries no astronauts or cosmonauts.

RETROFIRE: When a spacecraft turns backward and fires its engine in front of it as it flies. It is used to slow the spacecraft down.

ROCKET: a projectile that can shoot a spacecraft into space by igniting its combustible fuel

ROLL: when the spacecraft moves the way a can or other cylinder does if you lay it on its side and give it a push so it rolls along the floor

SATURN V: massive, thirty-six-story, three-stage rocket that would blast the *Apollo* spacecraft moonward

SOLAR PANELS: Winglike structures attached to a spacecraft. They are covered with solar cells that absorb sunlight and convert it to electricity.

SOLID-FUEL ENGINE: a rocket engine using a rubbery fuel that looks a little bit like a pencil eraser

SOYUZ: A Russian spacecraft capable of carrying up to three people. It was first used in 1967 and is still being used today. The same name is used to refer to the rocket that carries the spacecraft to orbit.

THRUSTERS: Little engines positioned on the outside of a spacecraft. They help it maneuver in different directions.

TITAN: rocket that launched *Gemini* spacecraft

UMBILICAL: the safety cable that attaches a spacewalking astronaut to the spacecraft

VELOCITY: speed

YAW: when the nose of the spacecraft waggles left or right; a

360-degree yaw would thus be a flat spin, moving around the way clock hands circle a clock face

ZERO-G: In space, astronauts feel no gravitational pull, which allows them to float. One g is the gravitational environment of the Earth.

INDEX